MW00559953

You Are Not Broken – How to Retrain Your Brain, Clean up Your Energy and Use Emotional Shapeshifting to Raise Your Vibration and Manifest Your Desires With Special Attention to Empaths and Other Highly Sensitive People

Rhonda Harris-Choudhry

Copyright © 2017 by Rhonda Harris-Choudhry

All rights reserved. No part of this publication either written or electronic may be reproduced, distributed, or transmitted in any form or by any means, including photocopying, recording, or other electronic or mechanical methods, without the prior written permission of the publisher, except in the case of brief quotations embodied in critical reviews and certain other noncommercial uses permitted by copyright law.

ISBN 978-0-692-12527-4

For permission requests, of if you want to contact the author, you may do so through her various links:

Her website where you can also download the free gifts mentioned in this book, set up readings, counseling, hypnotherapy and healing sessions, check out upcoming classes and find links to free video tutorials for empaths and spiritually minded people:
www.healinghennagoddess.com
Facebook: https://www.facebook.com/GoddessRhonda/
YouTube: http://www.youtube.com/user/Azjua7/featured
Email: goddessrhonda@healinghennagoddess.com

Acknowledgments

I am so grateful for my parents who taught me perseverance, my friends for supporting me and my trials for teaching me. I am so grateful for the wonderful teachers at the Hypnosis Motivation Institute for helping me to change my life and I am so grateful to the Most Holy and Divine Universal Life Forces who have guided me, protected me, taught me and kicked my butt to get this done. I am so grateful to Mark Stewart for being so instrumental in the editing, promoting and success of this book. Namaste and Blessed Be ♥

Table of Contents

Additional Alternatives to Visualization

Understanding the Lessons that Universe is Trying to Teach You
Acknowledge Your Strength
Energy Cleansing Step One:
Out With the Bad, In With the Good. How to Remove
Toxic Emotional Energy
Prep and Clean Your Vehicle
Pull Yourself Together (Literally)
Acknowledge Your Feelings
Validate Your Feelings
Release the Toxic Emotions
Get Into Your Element
Energy Cleansing Step 2 – Removing the Energetic Cords that Bind You
Quick Chakra Cleanse
Pink Lotus Realm Chakra Meditation
Program Your Chakras for Success
Energy Cleansing Step 3 – How to Call Your Purified Energy Back to You
Energy Cleansing Step 4 –Balancing the Body Mind and Spirit

Shields Up! How to Use Filtered Shielding to Protect You from Adverse Energies
Filtered Shielding
Solo Practice
Partner Practice
The Safe Space Shield
Energy Protection Gloves – Psychic Protection for Your Hands
Quick Grocery Cart Cleanse
Shielding Objects

How to Clear Your Home and Personal Spaces of Toxic Energy Debris
Cast the Negativity Into the Light
Quick Tips on Spiritually Cleansing Your Home
Full House Clearing Instructions

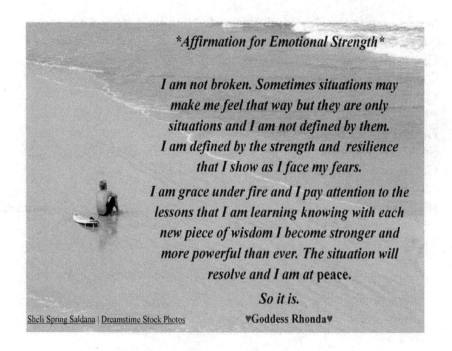

Affirmation for Emotional Strength

I am not broken. Sometimes situations may
make me feel that way but they are only
situations and I am not defined by them.
I am defined by the strength and resilience
that I show as I face my fears.

I am grace under fire and I pay attention to the
lessons that I am learning knowing with each
new piece of wisdom I become stronger and
more powerful than ever. The situation will
resolve and I am at peace.

So it is.

Sheli Spring Saldana | Dreamstime Stock Photos   ♥Goddess Rhonda♥

How this book came about

When I was a little girl, all I wanted to be for Halloween was a witch. My mother tried to get me to be a princess, a fairy, a ballerina but I just wanted to be a witch, and that was it. As a child I didn't really know what that truly meant, I just knew that was what I wanted to be. Now, of course, that translates as wanting to be a healer, to help others, live in harmony with nature, tap into the joyous energy of the Universe and be of good service to this world, which I have fully embraced. Light work, witchcraft, law of attraction practitioners are all very similar and use many of the same principles to try to heal, help and create better lives for others and themselves. This book was created to help all of the spiritual workers who toil so hard and manage to create for others but have such a difficult time creating for their own selves and can't figure out why.

I struggled with the same problem of manifesting what I wanted for myself but had no problem doing it for others. Many of the law of attraction books I read said it was all my fault and that I created the mess I was in which I felt was a load of crap and did not appreciate having blame and guilt heaped on my head when I was already feeling miserable over things it seemed I could not fix in my life. Did I make poor choices? Sure, but not all the time and many things that happened were out of my control. But even with the poor choices I had made, I finally figured out that they weren't all my fault because I was operating from adverse subconscious belief systems that were instilled in me as a child. I also discovered that I was so loaded down with toxic emotional and energetic debris that I was not aware that I was carrying from this and previous lifetimes. None of the information I read addressed this, nor did it give any techniques to fix it. I especially wanted and needed to know how to get rid of the toxic emotional and energetic debris that was flooding my system and may be flooding yours as well. This toxic energy may be severely affecting your ability to manifest things for your own use.

This book was also created in particular for empaths, a category of psychic healers that I also belong to. Back when I was a child, I didn't know I was an empath, one of the natural healers of the world. People, including adults, would tell me all of their problems even though I was just a child. My mother would witness this when she took me shopping. Whether she was trying on clothes or putting groceries in the cart, adults would come up to me to tell me their woes or ask my opinion about what they were buying. My mother marveled over this and could not figure out why people would not leave her child alone. I certainly didn't know what an empath was back then and I am sure she didn't either. Doing spiritual work and helping others became a natural part of my life. But helping myself? Not so much. When I was 16, my father bought me my first tarot deck which was truly out of character since my parents were staunch Baptists. When he gave them to me, he said he saw them in a store window and didn't know why he felt the urge to buy them for me, but he couldn't resist it. I still have that deck. Before my mother became ill, she studied herbalism and taught me about the healing powers of plants. I embraced those lessons and became so proficient at mixing them to heal others that my father began calling me his "witch doctor". I would help whoever needed it and because I opened those flood gates, I was also training myself to believe that the world's problems were bigger and more important than my own. I would place myself at the bottom of my priority list, if I even made it onto the list at all. I just loved helping people and still do except back then I did not know I was training my subconscious to accept the belief that neither I nor my needs were important and could wait while I tended to others. I had no idea that I was training my subconscious to accept this as my life script, a true belief that I was just not that important.

When I was 14, my mother became ill with heart problems and brain cancer and I took over my home, caring for her and my sister while my father worked three jobs to make up for the loss of my mom's income. I still had to get myself to school and do my own studies, but to me, my family's needs came first. This enhanced my empathic soul's belief of my duty to be of service to others. It also furthered my subconscious training of putting my needs last, but again I had no idea that this was happening.

I continued my metaphysical training, learning how to incorporate crystals, herbs, and energy to heal and help others. Helping others was my passion but helping me was not. This led to chaos in my personal life and because of my generous nature, led me to a lot of debt. I often gave whatever resources I had to those who I felt needed it more. Even when I did not want to do that, I couldn't help it thanks to being an empath and the extra training that my subconscious received throughout my life which was I am not important and others are more deserving.

While continuing my studies, I went into the mortgage business and became an underwriter. I made great money, but it went right out the window as I continued to help other people. Consciously, I could not understand why I was always in such an impoverished state. After all, I helped so many people to move forward in their own lives, to have wealth, a great career, good health but for some reason, I just could not manifest these things for myself. To be fair, I always had a roof over my head, clothes on my back and food in my stomach but I wanted more and just could not seem to get to the place I wanted to be financially. I had always heard that you get back what you put out, but that rule just did not seem to apply to me. I gave and gave yet when I put my hand out, no one was there. I became angry and bitter about it. I would rail at the Universe, asking why I had to struggle while those I helped were doing great. I did all kinds of manifestation work for myself, but still, while I was making a decent living, I just could not get out of debt and was always poised on the brink of financial disaster. In the meantime, I would create prosperity candles for others and money would come to them. I was baffled and the belief that I was just not worthy and that this was my lot in life became even more deeply cemented within me. After all, if I could dedicate myself to being of service and not get what I wanted back in return, then the Universe must not have wanted me to have those things, and I should just accept my lot in life. But I couldn't. I knew there had to be a way to fix my own life so I kept trying anyway.

Things got better for a while, but in 2005, my world turned upside down. In 2003, I accepted an underwriting job in New Mexico, grateful to get away from the NY winters. My husband and I loaded up the van and sallied forth with optimism. Even though we had no friends or family there, we had each other, so that was okay. Then came that fateful day in 2005, when I noticed that my husband's eyes looked jaundiced. I took him to the doctor that day and they immediately placed him in the hospital. Alas, we were too late. He had liver cancer and was given three to four months to live. After he accepted the diagnosis, he said he didn't want to hang around and deteriorate for three months. He was gone just two weeks after his diagnosis. He only waited for me to finish making his funeral arrangements, told me he loved me, said good bye and passed away. I was in complete states of both shock and loss and my stomach felt like I had swallowed bricks.

A month after he died, it began hurting so badly that I thought I had developed an ulcer and went to the doctor to get checked out. It turned out that I had a twenty pound uterine tumor that grew inward instead of outward, knocking my organs out of the way. The pain I was experiencing was because my organs had nowhere else to go. At first, the doctors thought that the tumor was cancerous, but thankfully it was a fibroid that had gone wild. The bad news was that my arteries had attached and it was expected that I would bleed out on the table. I told the doctor to sign me up for the surgery because I knew the Universe wasn't going to kill me. They were trying to teach me the huge lesson that I was so worried about everyone else that I didn't notice I was dying. Three months after the surgery, I returned to work only to lose my job two weeks later. It was the time of the decline and then crash of the mortgage industry. Needless to say, things got financially worse for me.

I was able to find another mortgage job but the company got sold three months after I started with them and their underwriting work was transferred to their main branch in New England. I was back on the streets again and unable to find another job except for some temp work. My house went into foreclosure and I managed to sell it 10 days before the foreclosure date but at a huge loss, so I barely got enough out to move. I lived off my credit cards for a while, amassing even more debt and sold off what little jewelry I had to help make ends meet. The final straw was when I had to sell my wedding bands, the last thing I had of any monetary value but priceless in emotional value. It was after that that I threw up my hands and surrendered it all to the Universe. I told the Universe that I was officially 30 days away from being homeless and asked what They wanted me to do. I was directed to take some of my money and buy copper wire to create copper and crystal bracelets for reiki healers.

I had studied reiki myself and thought that maybe this could work. After all, if I couldn't get back into the mortgage industry, I could utilize my metaphysical training and attempt to make a living at it. So with trepidation over spending even $50 for the supplies (copper was a lot cheaper back then), I went ahead and created the bracelets. I sent an email to every reiki healer in the area with a picture of the bracelets and waited for responses. I was nervous and excited at the same time. I received two responses. One said thanks, but no thanks and the other invited me to come show her my bracelets. Saying a million prayers that she would buy my bracelets, I trundled over to the then healing center, All Things Sacred and met with the owner Kathryn who purchased three of my bracelets after telling me I was selling them too cheap. She raised the price herself and then paid me that price. She then offered to allow me to use one of her rooms to do reiki and readings. I was stunned. This woman didn't know me at all but was generously offering me a place to work from. The room came with the massage table and chairs and all I had to do was bring myself. She also offered to refer clients to me and just like that, my business began.

Since she liked my bracelets, I decided to take them down to the local metaphysical store, the Blue Eagle, and asked the owner if perhaps he would sell my bracelets on consignment. As I was showing them to him, customers in the store came over and asked about buying them. The owner, Mitch, then offered to set up a little table for me in the store to let me sell my bracelets and do henna tattoos on the weekends. I couldn't believe my luck! I was so thrilled and saw things turning around for me.

From that point I began to build my business but as I was helping others to fix their lives as a professional spiritual counselor and psychic reader/healer, I still could not get out of debt. In fact, it got worse. I was baffled. Here I was, becoming well known for my skills at counseling, healing, and manifestation but I was still supplementing my food from a food pantry. I remember being thrilled to graduate to grocery shopping at the Dollar Tree. While I was grateful to see some progress, it was personally humiliating for me to be so poor while my customers were thanking me profusely for their new and better lives.

When all of the hoopla about the law of attraction began, I was fascinated by it. It encompasses the basis of witchcraft and light work intention manifestation, so it resonated with me right away. I hoped that maybe it had some extra wisdom to add to my knowledge and help me to help improve my life. I watched *The Secret* movie and read countless articles on it, but nothing changed for me. In fact, it actually hampered me because much of what I read flat out said that my issues were entirely my fault. It was my negative attitude, my poor choices, my "lack" mentality that had landed me here and quite frankly, I resented that. After all, I certainly did not ask for all of the trials I endured. I didn't ask for my mother to have brain cancer so I could willingly give up my childhood. I didn't ask for my husband to die, to grow a 20 pound tumor, have the mortgage industry crash, lose my home, etc. At that time, I did not yet know that I was an empath, nor did I know about my subconscious training.

I also found it frustrating that visualization is called for in just about everything I had read and alas, I was not a visual person, at least not at the time. Thankfully I've gotten much better at it but at the time, not being able to effectively visualize what I wanted made me feel more like a failure.

I decided to take a hypnotherapy course so that I would be able to do past life regressions and to help people with various phobias and challenges as a part of my practice. It was through that course that I learned about the subconscious, how it rules 88% of what we do and is typically trained during our childhood, creating a life script that results in subconscious behaviorism based on the conditions we were raised in. It was a true "AHA!" moment for me. It was such a relief to know that I was not consciously making the decisions that put me where I was. I was at the whim of my subconscious behaviorism based on the life script that was formed during my childhood. In order to change my subconscious behaviorism, I had to retrain my subconscious. I created self hypnosis scripts for myself and also used hypnosis to help my clients. Things got a bit better but definitely not enough. There was still something wrong.

It wasn't long after that by chance I saw an article on empaths. I can't remember exactly how or why it popped up on my search engine, but I am sure the Universe sent it to me. I was completely blown away as I read the traits of an empath and saw myself in just about every one of them. What I couldn't find were ways to help me both embrace and navigate my way through my powerful need to be of service while also being of service to myself. That was when I asked the Universe to teach me how to help myself and other empaths and They did. They channeled exercises and lessons to me which I tried on myself and could not believe how much better I felt and how much more self-productive I became. Of course, now I had a new mission which was to help other empaths and spiritual workers to understand their gifts and to teach them how to set boundaries and to tend to their own wings. I asked the Universe to send me these people as clients so that I could teach them and the Universe obliged. But now I had to balance my new need to help other empaths with my need to help myself. It is something that I have to stay on top of constantly. Thankfully, all of the techniques I've learned from Deity, my hypnotherapy, my reiki training and all of the other knowledge I have amassed, has steadily helped me to do this.

Finally, after much frustration and disappointment, I realized that I was not the broken one. These systems do work but not in a generalized way. I set to work customizing my own programs and they finally began working for me. They worked so well that I decided to write some articles about how to customize the system back in 2013 and published them in *Light Worker's World*. I began to call myself a Goddess because I realized that if I could subconsciously create chaos in my world, then I could certainly consciously create balance, peace, and prosperity. I created a *YouTube* channel to help teach other spiritually gifted people. I've taught many empaths and other beautiful spiritual people who want to help others and themselves. I decided to write this book to help as many of the heart-based, giving and beautiful spiritual beings that populate our beautiful earth that I can. I've incorporated videos for those who like to learn visually as well as visual aids for those who are not visual. I've also addressed empaths in many sections since they have specific needs. I've also taught how to customize the programs so that they work with you and not against you.

If you know of others that this book may help, please refer them to it. May this book truly help you become or attain that which you desire.

One last thing, I give a lot of exercises in this book, and while I hope they help everyone, I don't expect everyone to resonate with everything I have written or all of the exercises. Please do try all of the exercises just once and make a note of the ones that do help you. Also feel free to incorporate your own techniques since it is very important that all of the work that you do is custom to your personal belief systems. If you are having difficulty manifesting love, prosperity or whatever it is that would bring you the happiness you seek and would like to set up a session with me, you can contact me at www.healinghennagoddess.com or through my email address:
goddessrhonda@healinghennagoddess.com

Namaste and Blessed Be - ♥Goddess Rhonda♥

Freeimages.com/Anders Engelbol

CHAPTER 1

Why Not Me?

The Law of Attraction (LOA) really does work, so why isn't it working for you? It can be quite frustrating to listen to the success stories of others, how they managed to overcome illness or poverty or whatever it was they felt was holding them back and all you got from the exercise was, well nothing. Or, perhaps it has worked for you in the past but not in your present circumstances and you're stumped as to why. The short answer to that is most law of attraction programs are generalized with the hope that it will fit most of the needs of others, the keyword being most. As I always say, "we are not cookies made from the same cutter", so generalized methods may not work for your custom situation.

No worries! This book will teach you how to design a custom law of attraction system that will work with your unique circumstances to help bring you what you want and get you on the road to success in no time.

One of the keys to mastering the law of attraction is by consciously raising our vibrational frequency so that we aren't dwelling in the doldrums of poverty, depression, and the chaotic lower energies around us. Some of the steps we are to take to achieve this is through:

> ➢ Clear intentions
> ➢ Visualization
> ➢ Maintaining positive thoughts and emotions to raise our vibrational state.
> ➢ Believing that what we are trying to manifest has already happened before it actually does.
> ➢ Believing that what you receive in life is the result of the type of energy you put out. Thus we must change our energy output to constantly reflect happiness, wealth, love and success, etc.

The danger in generalizing these programs is that they do not take into consideration the specific needs and skills of the person trying to make the system work for them. That means you. Because of this, many people may actually end up feeling worse when trying these programs because they can't seem to take the required steps to realize their dreams. So what goes wrong?

Making sure that your intentions are clear is extremely important. After all, if the Universe does not fully understand the request, you may not get what you want. It's not enough to just say that you want a new job or a new love in your life. It has to be broken down further, such as what kind of job? Or, what kind of person are you trying to attract? If you have stated intentions without breaking them down to the finest details, don't feel bad about this. You probably weren't taught to do this, but that fact is about to be remedied. We will discuss more about setting clear intentions in chapter 11 so that the Universe will know exactly what it is that you want and will fulfill it for you.

Another of the most crucial components of most law of attraction programs is visualization. But what if you can't visualize? Not everyone is visual, particularly empaths who tend to be more "feeling". It can be a miserable experience to sit through a guided meditation with lots of visual references of beautiful meadows and peaceful oceans, seeing those around you smiling and engaging in the serenity these pictures bring them and all your mind comes up with is a blank screen.

To make things worse, not being able to visualize what you need may add to feelings of failure and frustration, emotions that can severely compromise your efforts to succeed. We will discuss how to get around visualization in chapter 4.

It is also considered imperative that we keep our thoughts and emotions positive at all times so that the vibrational frequency that we are putting out is one that is conducive to attracting and receiving good things. It is a belief that our mental and emotional states determine what we attract into our lives. This is only partly true because it is actually your subconscious that greatly determines what you are attracting (which will be discussed more fully later in this book). Still, it is definitely beneficial to stay immersed in positive thoughts and feelings. If you are one of those people who are naturally optimistic, this will be a cake walk for you, but for others, it can be a bit of a challenge to keep positive thoughts in mind when you don't have the money to pay your bills and feed your family.

Believing that you already have all of the money that you need while pulling a stack of collection notices out of your mailbox is not an easy thing to do either. Neither is believing that you already have the job of your dreams when you are calling in for your unemployment benefits. Fighting off desperation, depression and or anxiety caused by your situation is hard enough. Seeming to constantly lose the battle can also add to your feelings of failure because after all, how hard can it be to visualize and stay positive? The truth is for many it's not as easy as it sounds.

What about your life being a result of the type of energy you put out? Does that mean it's your entire fault that your life isn't going the way you want it to? Should you just be able to forget about all you have been through and are going through and just beam out positive energy and sunshiny thoughts?

Now on top of life seeming to be spiraling downward, you may feel guilty for not being able to *stop* feeling badly about your life which is then compounded even more by the feeling of perceived failure.

Empaths automatically carry inner guilt because they feel they aren't doing enough for others despite all of the good works they do. Add to that being told that it's all their fault that their lives are in such turmoil adds to that guilt, makes them feel worse and then wreaks havoc with their law of attraction system.

Taking these things into consideration, it is easy to see why the law of attraction system that was supposed to make your life better may make it seem much worse. You may sink even more into depression because you feel that things will never change and you are stuck with the cards you were dealt. Instead of walking with the confidence that you will achieve a much better life, you may be walking on tiptoe through what seems to be an endless field of land mines just waiting to blow up in your face from the slightest misstep.

This is not your fault. You are *not* broken, but your law of attraction method *is* because it is not customized to for you.

There is also another *HUGE* factor that may have ruined your chances before you even got started and that is that ***no one told you how to first prepare for your new journey.***

Check and clean your soul's vehicle
It's not wise to go on a long road trip without first making sure your car is ready for the journey. Typically, we clean out the car, maybe get an oil change and make sure all the fluids are topped off, there's enough air in the tires and the brakes are in good shape. Our bodies both physical and energetic are the vehicles for our soul. If you have been in a stressful situation for a period of time, many of your systems may be compromised. Physically you may feel drained, emotionally you may feel battered and energetically you may feel depleted.

Embarking on a new and greatly changing journey to freedom requires a well running and maintained vehicle to get you to your destination. You don't want to ride around in a vehicle that breaks down and leaves you stranded by the roadside hoping help will come along and drive you to safety. Chapter 5 will provide you with protocols to clear your energy and get your spiritual vehicle ready for the ride.

Make sure your spiritual GPS is up to date.
When beginning a new journey, we also want to ensure that we have an up to date map that will get us safely to our destination. GPS providers

make sure that their systems are always calibrated to the most recent road maps, so your journey will flow smoothly. We need to do the same thing but in a slightly different way. Our "old map" contains the lessons that our trials were supposed to teach us but somehow we missed. This is why we may start a new spiritual journey and end up right back where we started and not understand how that happened. We will discuss how to understand those lessons also in chapter 5.

We will also address additional but common reasons that can hinder your law of attraction efforts. Thankfully, there are ways to get around this that can help you to achieve the results you are striving for.

The Mighty Empath Also Known as Highly Sensitive People

Hail to the Mighty Empath!

A Super Hero with a sensitive nature but a core of steel
Has the strength to absorb the pain and aliments of
others to protect and heal them while still carrying on with their lives.
Incredibly psychic and able to feel even the most subtle
energies around them
Dedicated to being of service to help all living things
Puts the safety and well being of others before themselves
Where would the world be without you? Thank you for all that you do♥

For all of the empaths/highly sensitive people reading this book, you are rock stars, veritable superheroes! You have amazing psychic and healing abilities. You can sense and carry the pain and energy of others and still manage to multitask and try to help everyone. You are self-sacrificing in the interest of healing and helping others and take on your friends and families worries, shielding them as best as you can while confronting their issues for them. You are strong, resourceful, caring and generous, certainly worthy of more than you allow yourself to receive. But because of your focus and dedication to others, you may have the hardest time of all trying to bring your own dreams to fruition. It's hard to manifest when everybody else's energy is in the way. You may have beaten yourself up for spending so much time helping other people. You may have felt or been accused of being a pushover, but that's not true. The truth of the matter is that you don't just give of yourself because you hear a sad story. You give of yourself because you don't just hear the sad stories, you *feel* the pain of the storyteller. If they are speaking of the pain of their friends and or family members, you may feel that too. Their pain has become your pain so in trying to help them, you are stopping your own pain. It's almost a self-defense mechanism to just try to fix the situation before it gets further out of control, so you don't have to suffer anymore.

I truly believe that empaths are doing an angelic internship on earth and part of that training requires that we feel the pain of others because that pain inspires us to be of service to help the suffering which is a lot of what angels do. Still, it's important that we also focus on our own journey and that which we want to achieve. These lessons are also geared to help the empaths who need the knowledge and that extra push to balance out their lives and get on their own priority list. Please pay particular attention to the lesson and exercises in the How to Remove the Cords that Bind You section in chapter 5.

CHAPTER 2

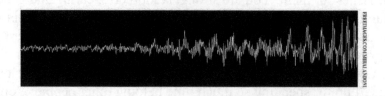

The Pre-Req's to Raising Your Vibration Through
Positive Thoughts & Energy

There are prerequisites to being able to raise your energetic vibration. These are:

1. Understanding how you got to this place.
2. Avoiding feelings of helplessness and failure.
3. Diagnosing and overcoming adrenaline addiction.
4. Mitigating self-induced "bad karma" from guilt carried over from the past.
5. Addressing shame and feeling worthy of receiving what you want.
6. Ceasing to give your energy away through envy.
7. Recognizing that you are golden.
8. Being honest with yourself about your wants and needs.
9. Embracing change.

Some of these you may have already worked on and mastered, but there may still be other issues that you need to address for a full emotional energy makeover. This chapter will cover each of these topics to help you to understand and release them so you can get on with achieving your goals and dreams.

1. Understanding how you got to this place
Understanding how you got on the path to your trials and tribulations can go a long way in helping you defeat the adverse situations you are in. This wisdom may also help you to avoid the same pitfalls in the future and to maintain a positive attitude since maintaining that positive attitude is a key to getting what you want. I want to reiterate that ***it is not your fault*** if you have not been able to maintain a positive state of being.

You have three major opponents that are effectively blocking you from keeping a happy state of mind and energetic outflow. These are:

- Life
- Your Subconscious
- Your Emotions

All three of these are entwined and work together to create the not so great situation that you may be in.

Life

Life happens and presents us with situations that we have no control over. The recession that may have cost you your job was not your fault and the Universe didn't cause it to just to screw up your life. That's something you can thank the politicians for. If you are battling an illness of your own or for a loved one that wiped out your savings or has drained you of energy and optimism, that is also not your fault. These were things that you had no control over and recognizing that can help you to release any thoughts of bad luck or persecution with the realization that unfortunately, things happen. The most important thing to remember is that you CAN mitigate and perhaps even heal these situations by utilizing the law of attraction to bring you good health or that better job. Once you get into the right frame of mind and the right energetic state, things will begin to improve. Let's move onto the subconscious.

The Subconscious - the Ruler of Your Actions

One of your biggest opponents to success is your subconscious. Even though we think we know what we are consciously doing, it is our subconscious mind that is typically calling the shots. It rules 88% of what we do and is constantly working in the background to either help or hinder us. Which one it does depends on how it was trained.

The subconscious does not know the difference between what is right and wrong. It only knows what is "normal" and then will fight like hell to keep things in that "normal" state. It will set floors and ceilings that allow you some leeway but not much. Let's take a look at some examples of this.

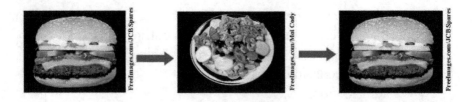

Let's say you weigh 150 pounds and have weighed that for some time. This is the weight that your subconscious now accepts as normal. You decide to adopt a healthier lifestyle and want to lose 20 pounds and get into better shape. So you change your meal plans, begin exercising and start seeing results.

Now let's say you lost the 20 pounds and are feeling great about seeing the magic number 130 on your trusty scale. Your clothes fit better, you're receiving lots of compliments and congrats on your success and life seems great. But despite enjoying these happy feelings and being in better physical shape, your subconscious goes into a panic and responds with, "What are you doing? We've weighed 150 pounds for some time, it's normal for us, so we need to go back there." Suddenly you don't feel like exercising as much and the chocolate addiction you thought you'd successfully beaten is now back with a vengeance. You succumb to your desire for sweets or heavy foods or whatever your culinary preference is, and the weight begins to creep back up. Even though you see this increase when you get on the scale and feel it when you try to zip up your jeans, you still can't stop your journey back to weight gain.

Now let's say you've eaten your way back to 150 pounds but don't stop there. Your food addiction has taken over, you've stopped being active and your weight blossoms to 170 pounds. Again your subconscious goes into a panic and responds with, "Haven't we talked about this? We are supposed to weigh 150 pounds and now we're up to 170. It's time for you to start dieting again and get back down to the 150 pounds we are used to." Now you get off the couch and start walking again and trim down your eating habits to get you back to 150 where you continue to hover and try though you will, you can't seem to break this cycle.

The same rule applies in just about any area of your life where you can't seem to make the changes you need to have a better life.

Let's take a look at another example:

The Cycle Continues

Let's say you've been in a state of financial distress for some time now and you've been working your LOA program to bring in greater wealth. You've been able to make gains and bring in extra money that should help your situation, but as soon as the money comes in, something happens that takes it right back out of your wallet and you are left exactly where you started off or in even worse shape. Again, this is your subconscious working its own law of attraction techniques to attract situations that keep you in financial distress because it feels that's what's normal.

You might even manage to get a better job that should handle things nicely, but just after you start receiving your new and greater paychecks, a new and greater expense enters your life. Perhaps your car dies and you have to buy a new one which means a hefty car payment and the resulting heftier car insurance that eats up your new salary and once again you're struggling. This is because your subconscious sets floors and ceilings in just about every area of your life including your finances and will try to keep things "normal". This means every time you've launched an intention, you did it from the emotional platform your subconscious has set for you.

So how does the subconscious determine what is normal? To be fair, your subconscious doesn't just decide to accept those things that are adverse to you as normal. It takes time for it to analyze what is normal for you based on what you have experienced for a prolonged amount of time and your reactions to the situation(s). You probably know of, and may be envious of, those who seem to float through life without a care in the world with plenty of money, great jobs and the air of happiness that comes with these things. If having these great benefits are normal for them, then their subconscious accepts that and keeps the good things coming. They may have grown up in a wealthy environment or just one of happiness and support which becomes the life script that their subconscious follows. However, should these blessed people suddenly find themselves in dire straits for a prolonged period of time, their blessed normal state can take a plunge and their subconscious can convert their normal state into one of need. How the subconscious works will be covered in more detail in chapter 8.

The important thing to know right now is that the adverse patterns in your life that you can't seem to break free from are just symptoms of your true challenges which are the false beliefs your subconscious holds about what should be "normal" for you. Hopefully now you can see why just changing your thoughts is not enough. What you really need to change is your subconscious behaviorism which, believe it or not, can be done. It takes effort but at least now you will have some tools that can truly help you instead of advice your subconscious has no intention of taking, that being think happy thoughts all the time.

If you badly injure your knee and just take pain killers for it that will help with the pain but doesn't fix the problem. You still have to address the real challenge which is getting the knee back in shape with surgery or rehabilitative therapy. The subconscious is no different. Trying to constantly think happy thoughts is the equivalent of just taking pain killers for a bad knee. In order to create true change in your life, it's time to do some rehab therapy on your subconscious. In chapter 3 we will start looking at how to achieve this using some of the natural tools we were given to keep our subconscious trained to help us instead of harm us. These tools are our attention and our *alarm emotions* which are then combined with understanding the lessons we have learned from the past.

Alarm emotions are those feelings that let us know something is wrong and needs to be attended to such as fear, depression, anxiety, sadness, etc. They sound off all the time and the trick is to pay attention to them and take action to end the perceived emotional and even physical threat. These emotions are not here for us to wallow in and allow to consume us. They are here to let us know something is wrong and needs to be fixed. Exercises to help you release these alarm emotions and healing the energetic harm they cause will be given in chapter 5.

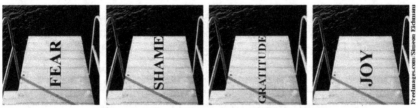

What's Your Emotional Platform?

2. Avoiding feelings of helplessness and failure -

You already know how awful it is to feel helpless to change your personal situations. Feeling helpless to change an outcome may also bring feelings of failure due to your not being able to stop it. These feelings can become even worse when we allow outside factors into our lives that can exacerbate our feelings of helplessness and failure such as:

A. **Watching the news first thing in the morning -**
Watching the news first thing in the morning can really get you off to a bad start by setting the tone and energy of helplessness and futility right at the start of your day. If you are already experiencing feelings of futility and helplessness over the situations in your own life, one of the very worst things that you can do is to watch the news first thing in the morning when your defenses are down and you are more susceptible to adverse energies. If you just have to know what's going on in the world, read a newspaper instead. Here's why:

The news is filled with details of the horrors, pain, and suffering that people are going through. Subjecting yourself to watching news footage videos of the painful happenings going on in the world that you have no control over can start your day off with feelings of helplessness and failure as you listen and watch atrocities that you feel you have no power to stop. These feelings can permeate your whole day.

Watching the news on your television or electronic device also adds other levels of sensory awareness that reading a newspaper doesn't. You hear the newscasters telling the stories and showing pictures of war-torn areas and the people suffering in them. You listen as they describe senseless criminal acts in dramatic tones and see footage of crime scenes with grieving families. The sadness that comes with these stories just adds to the feelings of powerlessness over not being able to help these people facing such tragic events in their lives. *Empaths especially may feel the energy of the newscaster, the pain of the grieving families, etc.*

Each new story that you watch during the broadcast adds additional alarm emotions that piggyback the ones caused by the preceding story. By the time you finish watching the news, you could be operating on an adverse form of sensory overload, feelings of being powerless and ultimately failure as you are made witness to situations that you have no way of fixing. Now you could be launching your day from an emotional platform of futility which can seriously hamper your energetic frequency and your LOA efforts. *The adverse effects of this are even worse for empaths and other highly sensitive people.*

Even worse, it can train your subconscious to focus on the "negative". The subconscious is very open to suggestion first thing in the morning and just before you go to sleep. By watching the news first thing in the morning, you may be teaching your subconscious that it is "normal" for you to focus your attention on negative situations and to feel helpless to boot. This could be just one of the reasons why so many people focus on the adverse situations in their own lives which can eclipse all of the many blessings that are surrounding them. For example, you may know someone who is having a bad relationship issue and that's all they focus on. This person may have everything else going for them such as a great job, financial security, a beautiful home, great health, etc. but all they are focused on is the one area of their life that they feel is lacking. There are exercises at the end of this section that are designed to help you to focus on the positives, the many blessings in your life, instead of those few lacking areas that you may be having such a hard time tearing your attention from.

If you are one of those people that like to know what's happening, consider reading a newspaper on your lunch hour instead. Even with e-newspapers, you can pick and choose what you expose yourself to by looking at the headlines and avoiding stories detailing the pain of others. It gives you a level of control that watching the news can't give you. Even if you just can't stop yourself from reading some of the horror stories, you can at least avoid being exposed to all of them as well as the sensory overload that can come from watching broadcast news.

Another reason you may focus on that one area of your life - I know that there may be many empaths and other highly sensitive people who may have read the above and feel guilty for focusing on the lack in their lives instead of their blessings. Please don't feel bad about this. Aside from the other reasons that will be addressed later in this book, there is also a big spiritual reason. The Universe is trying to get you to learn an important lesson from this trial and will keep bringing your attention back to it until you resolve it and learn the lesson. There are no mistakes, there are only lessons and while the Universe does want you to focus on resolving and learning from whatever issue you are going through, it also wants you to be aware of all of the good things going on in your life as well so that you have not only emotional balance but recognize that the Universe is not against you, which is what it can sometimes feel like after going through a struggle.

B. Avoid going on social media first thing in the morning -
Raise your hand if one of the first things you do when you get up is head over to your favorite social media site to see what's new (my own hand is raised). Social media may contain all sorts of amusing pics and posts from your friends and family and it's fun to check in and see how and what everyone is doing. But interspersed between the hilarious memes, family photos and endearing videos of cats, dogs and babies are also pleas for help, news of illness or tragedies that have happened to friends or in some other part of the world. Once again, feelings of helplessness can arise. The good news is that your trusty mouse gives you the power to pick what you want to be exposed to. You can scroll right past the things that may upset your day and lower your energetic vibration.

C. Remember that you are not as helpless as you feel -
Your feeling of helplessness is just an illusion because there is always something you can do. You can pray for relief for the victims of tragedy, donate money to their cause, send peaceful and healing energies to comfort them and hopefully bring a quick resolution. You can light a candle with the intention that it sends healing energy to the sick or justice to the violated. Just sending thoughts of love and peace may help not just them but help you as well as you recognize that you can do something no matter how small. The extra added benefit to this is that as you start doing these things to help others and feel better because of it, it may give you the incentive to do the same things for yourself to start healing your own situation from a platform of hope instead of helplessness.

3. Are You an Adrenaline Addict?

Adrenaline addicts are not just people who like to ride all of the most heart-stopping rides in an amusement park or jump out of airplanes and engage in other high-risk adventures. Adrenaline addicts can also be everyday people who have experienced a prolonged period of stress due to traumatizing situations. Prolonged stressful situations can put us in survival mode and cause adrenaline to course through our bodies to ready us for fight or flight. The adrenaline rush and resulting release of dopamine can become so addictive that even after the situation is resolved, the body still craves it. This can cause you to subconsciously create new stressful situations to keep the adrenaline flowing or cause you to continue to wallow in memories of that situation that you just can't seem to let go of. It can also put the nix on your manifestation work because it can create an adverse emotional platform that you are launching your intentions from.

Even if you are not thinking of things that cause the adrenaline to rise, it may rise up anyway without provocation. You could be just sitting on the couch watching television and suddenly feel anxiety creeping up and taking over, perhaps turning into a full-fledged anxiety attack. That is your body getting its adrenaline and dopamine fix. It is the equivalent of a drug dealer showing up at regular intervals to give their favorite addict their fix, of course at a great cost. Adrenaline addiction can cause dangerous physical health problems as well.

Cortisol –
Cortisol goes hand in hand with adrenaline and is also known as the stress hormone. Prolonged elevated levels can cause a myriad of physical problems such as heart disease, high blood pressure, diabetes. It can also pack on the belly fat and keep you from losing weight. If you are prone to stress and have a large amount of excess belly fat that won't go away, it may be time to see your doctor, have your levels checked and discuss ways to lower them.

It's not that long ago that I found out that I am an adrenaline addict. I became an adrenaline addict when I was a child, but you can become one at any age. My mother became very ill when I was 14, and I had to take over my household to care for her, helping to raise my younger sister while getting myself through school. This put an enormous amount of stress on me and my childhood went right out the window. Because of the pressure of caring for my mother, my sister and myself and trying to juggle everything successfully, I had adrenaline coursing through me on a regular basis as I tried to keep up with my own schoolwork, cook, clean, take care of my mother, and help my sister with her schooling, etc.. This helped to teach my subconscious that care giving and functioning under high-pressure situations was normal. This was compounded by watching my father work three jobs to make up for the loss of my mother's income, get her to her doctor's appointments or visit her every day in the hospital where she would stay for months at a time, and his struggle to pay the bills and seemingly live without sleep. Because much of our life script can be based upon watching our parents and how they deal with situations, seeing my father struggle under enormous responsibility enhanced my subconscious' growing belief that struggle, pressure, caregiving and persevering through the worst of circumstances was "normal". Being an empath put the cherry on the cake and a workaholic, type "A" personality, caregiving, chaos creator, back to the wall, "grass is greener" mentality, adrenaline addict was born. I use grass is greener as in the saying "the grass is always greener on the other side of the fence" because I couldn't stop wondering why everyone else's life seemed so much better than mine. That saying should be corrected to the grass always *seems* greener on the other side of the fence because as I got older, I realized that everyone has issues to deal with.

Thanks to this pre-adult training, I spent most of my life seeking out people to care for, creating chaos through procrastination so that I was always working under duress while being proud of my ability to work so well with my back against the wall. Financial stress was a way of life, and I am sure I created much of it to help keep the adrenaline flowing and also because it was "normal" for me. My body became its own drug dealer.

Struggling under so much pressure at an early age also taught me to be solitary because I had no one I could talk to about these things. I didn't talk about it much with other kids because I didn't think they would understand especially, since they spent lots of time making fun of my worn shoes and clothing and not inviting me to their social functions because of my impoverished state which made me shy away from being around them even more. Teenagers can be extremely cruel and many of the ones I went to school with were no exception. But even when I was with my true blue friends, I still didn't feel like I could truly talk to them because we were on such different mental planes. While they were concerned with going to the mall and buying the latest fashions, I was concerned with getting home before my younger sister so I could care for her and make sure my Mom was fed and cared for as well as keeping up with my own studies. This caused me to emotionally isolate myself from others.

We were also under orders not to give my mother any reason for concern, so I learned to just suck things up and keep my problems to myself. This created not just the subconscious belief that I had to take everything on alone and caused an inability to ask for help but also added to my adrenaline habit thanks to the pressure of feeling I had to take on the world alone. There were other consequences from my childhood that will be addressed later.

Causes: Adrenaline addiction can be caused by a prolonged period of stress. The recent recession may have created more adrenaline addicts because many feared not having a job and may have become even more desperate after losing their jobs and unemployment benefits. Some people go through life- threatening illnesses or have to care for someone who is battling for their life. Some people may also have a natural tendency towards it. They may have a need to achieve or become fire fighters, police, join the military, do stunt work for movies or engage in any number of high-risk practices. While I am an adrenaline addict, I am not an expert or a medical professional. However, there is a lot of information about adrenaline addiction on the internet, and you should ask your doctor about it, particularly a mental health professional if you feel you may be one. You can also speak to a spiritual counselor and/or hypnotherapists to learn new ways to control your stress. The resource section of this book contains several articles on the subject that you might find helpful.

Some symptoms of being an adrenaline addict. You don't have to experience all of them to be an addict:
- ✓ Constantly adding more tasks to your to do list even though you already feel overwhelmed.
- ✓ Engaging in the dramas of family members and friends to the point that you feel their problems are yours.
- ✓ Feeling the need to engage in high-risk behavior, jobs, etc.
- ✓ Having a deadline and procrastinating until it is almost time for the project to be due.
- ✓ Having difficulty doing one thing at a time.
- ✓ Having difficulty finishing a project because so many other things pull you away from it.
- ✓ Ending the day by adding to tomorrow's to-do list.

- ✓ Lack of concentration
- ✓ Often feeling on the verge of a panic attack or having panic attacks
- ✓ Difficulty relaxing
- ✓ Having a need to be doing something most of the time
- ✓ A large amount of belly fat

Overcoming adrenaline addiction:
I sought therapy for my adrenaline addiction and was taught by my therapist to become mindful of my body and mental state. This was very helpful because I began to notice when the adrenaline was starting up. I can actually feel it as it begins to flow. My therapist taught me to stop it by breathing and focusing on something else. The first thing she said for me to do is when I feel the rise of adrenaline, look for five round blue things in the room I am in. One evening after I felt it coming on, I started looking around my room for five round blue items. I didn't think I had five round blue items but looked anyway. To my surprise, I had more than five items. What's even better is that after I had finished counting them, I felt so much better and the adrenaline feeling was gone. I also use this technique while driving. If I feel the adrenaline starting to flow, I count how many red pickup trucks go by or how many beige cars, etc. I also created emotional freedom tapping and self hypnosis scripts to calm me down further. I have had much success in teaching emotional freedom tapping to my clients as well as using hypnotherapy to help them to calm down. In chapter 14, we will discuss using color therapies to help change your mood and energetic vibration.

Doing something physical such as exercise can help and so can deep breathing and meditation. Try different techniques and see which one works best for you since different things work for different people. If nothing else, at least you may now have a better understanding as to why your LOA techniques don't work if you are an adrenaline addict. In chapter 5, I will show you how to transmute anxiety and even depression into pure energy and infuse it with positive intentions. You might as well make it work for you instead of against you.

4. Is your past life affecting your current life?
It is not uncommon for people to come into this life carrying the burdens of past life issues. Empaths and other people who have embraced

spirituality and service to others in this life were also often people who were the same in other lives but in the form of priests, nuns and other spiritualities that may have required them to take vows of poverty, celibacy, etc. Empaths particularly embody being of service to others even to their own detriment which can also be an offshoot of being a High Priest or Priestess, the community healer or spiritual advisors to royalty. You may have practiced Buddhism or Hinduism and taken the Bodhisattva vow which is a vow to put all others before you and to continually come back and be of service until everyone reaches enlightenment. Sound like an empath? Yes, it does. It also sounds like others who have similar beliefs within other forms of spirituality. Your soul is the same soul that it was in past lifetimes so if you took a vow in another lifetime, depending on how it was worded, it may still be affecting your ability to manifest what you want in this lifetime. This includes vows of poverty. If you are trying hard to consciously manifest money but keep finding yourself struggling financially, you may have taken a vow of poverty that your subconscious remembers well and is still holding you to it.

Vows from past lifetimes can also be affecting your love life. Let's say that in a previous lifetime you loved someone very much and vowed to love them until the end of time. That vow can still be holding you back from finding real love in this lifetime. You may feel like a piece of you is missing as you long for someone whose name you may not remember and look for that person in everyone you date only to find them all lacking. If you took a vow of celibacy, this too can interfere with your love life or make you feel guilty about sexual relations so that you never truly relax and enjoy sexual intimacy.

Renounce the vows-
If the above rings true to you, then you may want to renounce that vow. Simply renounce the vow of poverty, chastity, bondage to old loves with the understanding that those vows are not applicable to who you are in this lifetime and what you want to accomplish. You can create a formal ritual for yourself or simply say something like, "I renounce the vow of poverty that I made in my previous lifetimes because it is not applicable to my lessons and evolution in this lifetime. I am now free to pursue and receive financial wealth in good conscience and with gratitude."

Now consciously renouncing the vow is easy but you need to check in with your soul to see how you truly feel about it. Do this by verbally renouncing the vow either out loud or silently and then wait a few moments to see if you feel an internal reaction. If you feel something akin to glee and freedom, then you are good to go. If you feel something like anxiety, fear, guilt, disappointment or any alarm emotion, then you may need to get some additional help to free you from this mindset that your soul has embraced. You can speak to your spiritual counselor, a mental health professional and/or a hypnotherapist. Hypnotherapists are also subconscious behaviorists and can help to implant new belief systems to replace the old outdated ones. We can also take you through past life regressions so that you can learn of how your past lives may be affecting this one.

You can also do healing and cleansing work on yourself if you are a healer/counselor. The important thing is to clear that mindset so that there is no conflicted energy in your manifestation techniques. Don't worry about the Universe or however you term Deity being angry with you for renouncing no longer needed vows. They understand that we are here to learn and evolve and will not hold you to an old vow that is keeping you from your lessons and evolution in this lifetime.

5. **Bad karma and how to mitigate feelings of guilt** –
It is not uncommon for people who may have had a misspent youth or even a misspent adulthood to feel guilty about those things they have done in the past, especially now that they have matured and recognized the error of their ways. This alarm emotion can become even greater if the person has become more spiritually enlightened. The feeling of guilt can wreak havoc with your LOA system as it also can flood you with feelings of unworthiness, shame, and low self-esteem. These are surefire LOA blockers.

Deeds from past lifetimes can also rear their heads here as well. I have had many very spiritual people tell me that they know they "screwed up" in other lifetimes by misusing their power, so they are walking around dragging their past life baggage of guilt and its accompanying friends- shame, unworthiness, and low self-esteem- with them.

Whether it's from your past life or your current life, these adverse emotions can cancel out your best LOA efforts by bringing on self-induced bad karma because you keep reminding yourself of the wrong you committed and wallowing in guilt. This type of guilt can underscore the feelings of unworthiness that will counter your best LOA efforts as well as impede your power. That is not to say that all bad karma is self-induced. Certainly, if a person has committed atrocious acts without repentance, the Universe is going to bring down the hammer to teach them a much-needed lesson. However, once a person recognizes their mistakes, takes responsibility for them and tries to make amends, the bad karma can be mitigated, and past offenses can be forgiven by the Divine. It's no different than when a person stands before the judge in a court of law, confesses and shows remorse. The judge may hand down a much lighter sentence to that person than one who stands arrogantly before them with no sign of contrition. We will discuss more about self induced bad karma through negative self talk in chapter 8.

Another reason that these memories keep coming up with the accompanying alarm emotions is to let you know that the adverse energies caused by the thoughts need to be purged from the body. When these memories come up, don't wallow in them. Instead say something like, "Thank you dear Universe (or however you term Deity) for letting me know I need to purge these feelings to restore my good health. I understand my lesson and now release these thoughts and accompanying adverse energies to you to be healed and recycled with my gratitude." Once you get rid of the energies of the past event, you will feel better and your system will finally get to heal.

There are many spiritualities that believe that if you ask the Divine for forgiveness, then forgiveness will be granted. Other spiritualities such as Hinduism offer ways to mitigate the damage done through chanting, prayer, and spiritual services. The point is that the Universe or however you term Deity can and will forgive you for past missteps. The most important thing is for you to forgive yourself.

The Universe understands that we are down here to learn and that we have to experience everything if we are to eventually become spirit guides/angels and be of service and support to the ones still learning on the earth plane. After all, it is probably easier to help an alcoholic if you were one yourself when you were on the earth plane. You will be better able to sympathize and empathize, understanding all they go through and you can use that understanding to help guide them to sobriety as one of the angels/guides assigned to them. The same is true for victims of terrible crimes. As an angel/guide who has lived through the horrors of murder, theft, and abuse, you can understand the pain of your Earth charges and help to guide them with understanding, love and patience as opposed to someone who has never experienced such awful things.

This is why the Universe can forgive you once you learn and accept your lessons especially if you apply those lessons to help others. The problem comes in when we can't forgive ourselves either consciously or unconsciously. This can cause us to become our own judge, passing down harsh sentences upon ourselves that can translate to poverty, illness, loneliness, etc. This can subconsciously keep us in the self-induced abyss that we are trying so hard to climb out of.

It's time to forgive yourself. If you are feeling guilty then you are probably recognizing and taking ownership of your mistakes. This means you have learned your lesson and can move on if you choose to. You may feel that what you have done is so awful that there is just no way to ever fix it. Guess what? You're right. You can't go backwards in time and fix it. But you CAN begin to make amends and resolve to "fix" your current situation and your future. Even if it takes three lifetimes to mitigate your deeds, you can still start now. Redemption is always before you with its hand out ready to take you under its wing and help you repair the damage or start fresh, but first, you have to begin the process of self-forgiveness to raise your level of self worth.

So how can we mitigate bad karma? Doing charitable acts with the conscious intention of mitigation can help you. When we do nice things for others, our self-esteem and sense of worthiness can get a boost. When you help someone, and they reward you with a sincere smile of gratitude, it can lift your mood and increase your sense of self value. The more we expose ourselves to this feeling, the more our subconscious will accept it as normal and a real positive shift can take place in your life. The trick is to consciously intend each act to be one of mitigation. So if you were to stop on the road to help someone fix a flat tire or let them use your phone to call a tow, make a conscious assertion that you are doing this to mitigate any bad karma you may have accumulated. It will help you to feel better knowing you are working towards redemption.

Here's the good news, you can get a massive head start on this if you pay taxes which you almost most certainly do even if it's just sales tax. Our tax dollars go towards health programs, schools and social services designed to help those in need. They help pay the salaries of law enforcement and fire fighters, keep the roads maintained so people can drive on them safely and fund the schools you're your children go to. This means you are already making charitable contributions with each paycheck, and every time you pay sales tax at the register. Even if you are handing over taxes unwillingly, someone still benefits so go ahead and claim that good karma. Each week when you look at your paystub:

1. Make the assertion that the taxes you are paying are to mitigate any bad karma by being allocated to help support our government systems, schools, and social services.
2. Take a moment to really recognize that because of the money you are providing through your taxes, that people will be helped because of it.
3. Next, allow yourself to feel grateful for being able to help others through your hard work.

Doing this provides you with many opportunities to mitigate your karma and can help alleviate guilt and raise your sense of self-worth and self-esteem.

6. **Addressing shame and feeling worthy of receiving what you want-**

In this section, we will discuss the importance of increasing your sense of self-worth which may have been remolded into feelings of shame and deficiency. As stated before, when using intention manifestation or law of attraction practices, conveying the proper emotion when stating your intents is essential. However, if you are attempting to bring extra money or love etc., into your life but deep down inside you don't truly feel worthy of receiving it, then your practices could amount to nothing. Even if you tell yourself you are worthy of receiving abundance in whatever area you wish, if your feelings of unworthiness have convinced your subconscious that this is true or "normal" then that is the energy that you will probably send out.

Give yourself a test by mentally making a statement and paying attention to your inner response. Let's say you want your business to take off. Mentally say, "My business is going to take off and be wildly successful." Then wait a moment to see if you get an inner response from your body such as happiness, optimism, fear, stress, any emotion or response that you may feel. Does your body relax or tense up? Does your breathing deepen or shorten? Some people may feel shame or embarrassment, especially if they were raised to believe that asking for wealth was akin to being greedy or that money itself is evil. If you were raised with that type of doctrine, your subconscious probably accepts it as true and can hit the brakes when you try to increase the flow of money in your life. The important thing to recognize is that the response that you get is how you truly feel about what you are trying to achieve. If you get a positive response like feeling happy and or uplifted, then you are good to go. If you feel any alarm responses to the statement of what you are trying to achieve, that tells what kind of energy you are putting into your work. It also points out what needs to be removed from your energetic system before doing intention manifestation work. Later, I will give exercises to help remove these energies from your system, but first, we need to explore the root of the problem.

So where does our sense of shame and unworthiness come from? It's not just about any anti-wealth religious doctrine that we may have been raised with or even abuse that you may have received as a child or even an adult if you have been in an abusive relationship. While these things can and usually do play a role and are things that need to be addressed and healed, much of this is caused by marketers that first play upon your perceived weaknesses and then try to convince you that they have just what you need to look and feel better about yourself. What they are actually doing is reminding you of how badly you should feel about yourself to get you to crave their "all fixing" products. In the movie the Silence of the Lambs, there is a classic question and answer quote summed up as," ...how do we begin to covet...we begin by coveting what we see every day...."

Every day the media inundates us with messages designed to make us feel deficient in some way. The Encarta Dictionary defines the word deficient as:

1. Lacking – lacking a particular quality, element, or ingredient, especially one that is expected or necessary
2. Inadequate - inadequate or not good enough

You need only watch television for an hour to be told that you are not skinny enough, buff enough, wealthy enough, your car is too old, your wardrobe is lacking, your eyelashes are too short, your hair is too thin, you have too many wrinkles and way too much gray hair. It's not just the television telling you this. Radio commercials hammer the messages into you as do the bill boards you drive past and even the internet. Go to your favorite site and chances are on the side of the web page, there are mini ads, some with video suggesting that you're too fat, under educated or it's easy to look better with some weird old trick. Translation: You are not good enough the way you are. You may not respond to all of these things but there's an excellent chance that internally, you are responding to at least some of society's propaganda that happiness lies in being young, slim, with long lashes and a scar and stretch mark free body or having muscular biceps, a hard 6 pack and driving the latest sports car. This is all on top of the programming that you may have received as a child.

Now there is nothing wrong with wanting a nice car or to get into shape but if you are struggling with your weight or just trying to have enough money to put food on the table and gas in the car, being flooded with images of size zero models, actors and actresses, luxury cars, homes, etc., may make you feel unworthy of having what you want especially if you have tried so hard to achieve them and have not been able to. The good news is that once you recognize how marketers have hoodwinked you into thinking that you aren't awesome just as you are, you can take steps to remove this energy from your system and restore your inner peace which we will discuss just a bit later.

7. **Keep your energy working for you and not those you envy.**
It's normal to be envious of those who seem to have what we are striving for and it's okay to use that envy as motivation to help you also reach your goals. However, if you find yourself spending an excessive

amount of time envying the fact that your best friend has such a great relationship and you don't or another friend has a great job making great money and you can barely pay your bills, you could be giving these same people the energy that YOU need to help boost you down the path to success. Every time you envy or give your attention to someone else's prosperity, *your energy is going towards their prosperity* which can help them but certainly not help you. If your thoughts are that Bob has so much money and is so fortunate, the energy of that declaration goes towards helping Bob keep his money flowing even as yours seems to dwindle. Whenever you admire your friend's awesome relationship, your energy is going towards their awesome relationship and not towards helping you find your own. If you think, Jane has such a great relationship, you are sending more energy to enhance Jane's great relationship.

Your thoughts and energy are extremely powerful and while it's nice to wish others well, it's important for you to refocus your energy back to where it belongs which is on your personal goals and dreams instead of lavishing it on others that already are doing just fine.

Add a postscript - If it's difficult for you to stop spending so much time on the blessings of others then after making the assertion that you are envious of what someone else has, add a postscript that sends the energy out for your own behalf. For example, "I'm so envious of my friend's great relationship, so I now direct my energy out to attract my new and wonderful love to me." Or if you are already in a relationship, "I now direct my energy out to help bring such happiness into my own relationship." Add this type of postscript whenever you feel envious over what someone else has to make sure your attraction energy is going towards your own benefit.

8. **Recognize that you are golden**
There may also be personal events that have happened in your life to instill these feelings of shame deep within you. If this is the case and you are having difficulty moving on, it's time to change your perspective about your worthiness. Don't allow your self-worth to be defined by people who just want to sell you their latest wrinkle cream. Believe it or not, back in the olden days there was a time when just your name or who you were as a person meant something. You may not have

had a lot of money but if you had a good name it was better than gold. When I was a child and did something wrong publicly, I would have to hear from my parents, "How could you do that? What kind of parent will the neighbors think I am? Do you want them to think I raised you this way?" My sister and I still joke about how we got in trouble more for the embarrassment factor as opposed to what we actually did. The translation of what my parents were saying was, you are ruining our good name.

When you strive to do the right thing, support your friends and family and provide a decent life for yourself and those you live with, you are already golden. You have honored the name of your parents and ancestors by living an honest life and being there for those you love. You do so much for so many people including you and should pat yourself on the back for it. However, before you can really reap the benefits of recognizing your self-worth, you must first be completely honest with yourself.

How Your Subconscious May See Your Conscious Mind

9. **Be honest with yourself about your wants and needs** One of the many things you may have been taught is to give without expecting anything back. Consciously, you may have adopted this belief and even pride yourself on your unselfish generosity. But this belief may be causing you problems on several levels.

A. When you assert this belief, you are telling the Universe that you expect nothing back and the Universe may very well say, "Okay" in response and not bother to bless you for your generosity.

B. If you don't truly believe this on your subconscious level, you are operating from a level of conflict. Not everyone has this conflict, and you will know if you do if when faced with an adverse situation you ask yourself or others, "I'm such a nice person, why does all this bad stuff happen to me?" By asking this question what you are really saying is, "I do a lot to help and bless others, why am I not blessed in return? Is it because I am unworthy? Why do others get to have help and I don't?" This is your subconscious belief of yes, I do deserve to be blessed for what I do and that's okay. Of course, you deserve to be blessed for all you do. The first step though is for you to accept what you truly believe which is that you do deserve to be compensated for the service you give to others. There are additional reasons that your subconscious may be calling you a liar which will be discussed more in later chapters.

Everything we do and think produces intention filled energy. If you have been putting your energy into feelings of unworthiness, you can take that same energy and shift it to help you manifest what you are trying to create in your life. We'll talk more about emotional shapeshifting in chapter 9 but for now, let's focus on your awesomeness!

Worthiness Exercise 1- Remind yourself of how awesome you are.
To help you to recognize your true self-worth, get a new notebook and before going to bed at night, write down the things that you did for yourself and for others, no matter how small or even if it is a part of your regular routine. It might be a part of your regular routine, but not everyone takes the time out to do caring things for their friends, family, and self.

Did you change a bunch of diapers today?
Take time out of your busy day to go to the grocery store, prepare food and feed your family?
Go to work even though you didn't feel like it?
Cart the kids to soccer practice/dancing lessons/boy or girl scouts, etc.?

Did you physically take your children to school to ensure their safety or walk them to the bus stop and wait for them to get safely on the bus?
Did you play with your children or just hang out with them?
Help them with homework?
Clean your home and do laundry for your family?
Are you in school or training?
Did you make someone smile today?
Did you make yourself smile today?
Did you help someone out in even the tiniest way?

These are all things that are reflective of being responsible, supportive and taking pride in doing good works for others and yourself. As you begin writing down all of the good things you have done for yourself and others every day, your sense of inner pride and worthiness will continue to develop. This way, when you do state your intentions, your feelings of self-worth will be sincere and intact and bring you closer to manifesting your dreams. Finish each day's entry with, as I have blessed others, so may I be blessed as well. I am worthy of all I desire and add your signature to claim it. This might feel uncomfortable the first few times but should become less so especially after you begin to reap the rewards.

Worthiness Exercise 2 – Count your blessings
Counting your blessings each day reminds you of how blessed you truly are which may then strengthen your sense of worthiness even more. It can also help you to change your perception of your situation by helping you see things in a more positive way. As I mentioned before, when I was growing up my family lived a regular middle-class lifestyle until I turned 14 and my mother became very ill and we lost her income. It started with heart problems then got worse with brain cancer and suddenly we were inundated with ongoing doctor and hospital bills. This plummeted us into *perceived* poverty which was bad enough but made even worse by those in our neighborhood who looked down upon us because of our reduced state of means.

Children, in particular, can be very cruel, and because I could not afford to buy designer jeans and hang out at the mall, I had who I thought were very close friends cut me out of their lives, stop inviting me to parties and pretty much treated me like a leper. When we are teenagers, it's normal to want to fit in and belong, but as an impoverished empath, that was not an option. I bring up my being an empath because not only did I suffer from hearing the whispers behind my back, I also felt the contempt that was being projected at me.

I hated not being able to buy and wear cool clothes and hated even more hearing the laughter and jokes about my old and worn clothes and shoes. It caused a great deal of heartache and low self-esteem and feelings of shame and unworthiness that I dragged into adulthood with me until I finally was able to put it in the rear view mirror where it belonged. I was able to do this when I realized that my "poverty" was a perception based on a comparison of what my peers had. As an adult looking back, I realized that while I didn't have the best clothes, I did have clothes. We always had food on the table, a roof over our heads and warm beds to sleep in. We had everything we needed, but in my child's mind at the time I didn't see that. All I saw was that everyone else seemed to have so much more and I felt like Cinderella with no Prince Charming in sight. That false belief impacted my life for many decades afterwards. I had to consciously change my perception of the past to keep me from continuing to drag it with me into my future.

I also try to count my blessings before I climb out of bed in the morning and when I climb back in at night. This helps me to both start and end my day in a positive state of mind and positive, energetic space.

Get another notebook and at the end of the day, write down everything you are thankful for. Start off with the basics and add to them.
Are you blessed with being able to breathe, even if you need an oxygen tank to do it?
Are you blessed with being able to walk or blessed with a way to get around?
Are you blessed with being able to speak or blessed with having a way to communicate?
Are you blessed with sight or have you been blessed with training for the sight impaired?
Are you blessed with being able to hear or have you been blessed with hearing aids or training for the hearing impaired?
Are you blessed to be able to go to the bathroom without the help of a dialysis machine?

If you utilize a dialysis machine are you blessed with having access to the services?
Are you blessed with a roof over your head?
Are you blessed with a bathroom to take a shower or bath?
Do you have running water?
Were you blessed with food today?
Do you have clothes on your back?
Do you have shoes on your feet?
Did you get to work safely?
Did you get home safely?
Did your family get to their destinations safely?
Did they return home safely?

The more you keep reminding yourself of how blessed you are, happiness can start to replace despair. Instead of feeling unlucky, you will realize exactly how lucky and blessed you are and how the Universe has supported you and your feelings of being supported and worthy of the even better things in life will increase. It helps to do this before you go to bed and when you first get up in the morning because the subconscious is more open to suggestion within 30 minutes of going to sleep and waking.

You truly are worthy of the life you want. Sometimes we all just need a reminder.

10. Embrace Change
Change can be scary on both a conscious and subconscious level. You might not be in the best of circumstances, but you are used to them, there's few surprises. Diving into the unknown can be as scary as jumping out of an airplane for the first time with just a parachute and hope to get you safely to the ground. As far as change goes, the thing to remember is that things are always changing and not always for the worse. Start thinking of change in terms of positive expectations and match your words to that intention. Instead of saying, If things don't change…", instill positive anticipation in your words by changing them to, "I am so glad that things are changing and I request and accept those positive changes I already know are going to transform my life for the

better." Smile, knowing those words are true and feel your frequency rise.

To help you accept and look forward to the new and positive changes about to arrive, try listening to my guided meditation:

Opening the Doors to New Beginnings

On your internet device, go to Blog Talk Radio at http://www.blogtalkradio.com and enter into the search, "Goddess Radio Opening the Doors to New Beginnings". The meditation will come up for you to listen and relax to.

CHAPTER 3

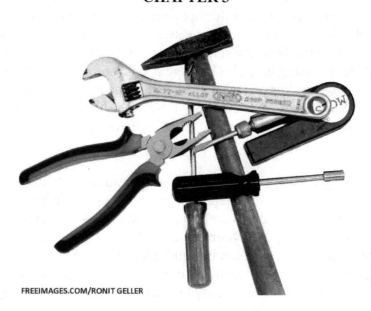

FREEIMAGES.COM/RONIT GELLER

How to Use Your Inner Tools and Why Self Centeredness is a Good Thing

One of the law of attraction's purposes of having to maintain happy thoughts is to help teach your subconscious a new "normal" by consciously creating a sustained level of peace within. As difficult as this may have been for you in the past, we are going to make it simpler by employing the tools you already have within you to make this happen. You have extremely valuable resources, veritable forces that can greatly influence your subconscious and change your subconscious behaviorism. *They are your attention and your alarm emotions.* Understanding how to navigate your emotions will be covered in chapter 5 so for now, let's start with your attention.

You have probably heard that where your attention goes, your energy flows. There is much truth to that. We can get so focused on the trials and pains of our families and loved ones or even the world at large that we don't notice what's going on in our own lives until things start to reach critical mass. That's when we are forced to pay attention, but things could've gotten so far out of control that they seem impossible to fix. This can be particularly true for empaths, healers, psychics and those in the healing/counseling industries because of all the sad stories we hear and energies we repair for our clients. Happy people don't normally consult spiritual counselors and healers. Few people will go to a psychic and say, "My life is so awesome, I just want to know how much more awesome it's going to get." These are people coming for help with serious issues and/or serious pain and since many healers and counselors are empaths as well, it can be easy to become so concerned for their clients they can end up dwelling in their clients' energetic realm of despair.

Consciously turning your attention toward yourself will allow you to notice the patterns in your behavior and what it is that triggers those behaviors that keep you where you are. Just understanding what is causing the challenges in your life is helpful. It's wondering why this is all happening to you that can be painful and produce feelings of not being good enough. By practicing **conscious self-awareness**, you can become mindful of situations at their start and work on resolving them before they get out of control.

But isn't it wrong to be self-centered? The answer is **NO** because you are not doing this with an "all about me" attitude. You are doing this because you are determined to create a better life for yourself which translates to a better life for your family and loved ones as well. Maybe you want to make more money to save for your child's education, or a new home or car. Maybe you want to lose weight or quit smoking so you can improve your health and live to see your grandchildren marry. There is nothing selfish in this at all because your efforts are also going to change the lives of your loved ones for the better with the extra added benefit of teaching those around you how to change their own lives by the examples you set for them.

Tend to Your Own Wings

If you go down, your ship goes down with you and then you *can't* help anyone else, let alone yourself. Therefore it is your duty to pursue your goals and dreams to fruition and practicing conscious self-awareness may be the key to finally get you where you want to be in life. If you are strong, healthy and successful, you can help those you care about. This is a far cry better than being stuck in the abyss with them without the strength to pull them or you out. As I always say, you can't help someone else fly if you have a broken wing yourself. Let's fix that wing so you can fly again and better help your family and loved ones to fly with you.

I have so much going on, how can I remember to focus my attention on myself?
This is actually quite simple since you have two internal alarms that frequently go off *to* get your attention in both of these areas and let you know that action needs to be taken. These internal alarm systems are your emotions and the incessant mind chatter that constantly reminds you of all of your obligations and questions you relentlessly about how you are going to fulfill them. Later we will discuss how to quiet the mind chatter. In the meantime, start off by working at your own pace.

If you can't do it for yourself, who can you do it for?
If you are having a difficult time putting your needs at the top of your priority list, don't beat yourself up. This is something that you can work on but in the meantime, if you can't do it for yourself then do it for someone love such as your children, your cat, your parents, all with the intentions of giving them a better life in some way. You still need to

work on yourself, either alone or with help but that doesn't mean you that you can't manifest what you want even though you are using someone else as your inspiration. Do what works for you.

What's your style? Toe in or all the way in?
Either way is fine as long as long as you are working at your own pace. When we discover a new program that promises to help change our lives, it can be very easy to plunge in and try to incorporate all of the suggestions at once. We do this because we want to quickly resolve our problems and for many, this immersion method works fine. But for others, this can cause us to burn out just as quickly. If you are the type that likes to slowly proceed, that's perfectly okay. You didn't get to this point over night so take your time. It's ok to take baby steps and ease into the program at your own pace, and it will probably end up working better for you since you are doing it within your own sense of timing.

Take 5 to patrol your soul's perimeters -
Taking 5 minutes to do a quick check on how you are feeling won't compromise your day and will let you know if you need to address anything. Just be still for a moment and ask, "How am I feeling?" and then pay attention. You may suddenly realize that you are tense and can take slow deep breaths to start to calm down. Even better, you may realize that you feel great which can make you feel even better. Depending on the custom way your body answers you, in your mind's ear you may get an auditory response. Others may "feel" the response in the form of an emotion. Still, others may get a physical response. Don't worry if you feel you didn't get a response. If you are new to energy work, translations may take time to figure out. The key is practice.

You can also do a simple shoulder test. When we are tense or upset, we may pull up our shoulders sometimes practically up to our ears. Take a slow deep breath in and as you exhale slowly, drop your shoulders. You may have to do this a few times to get your shoulders down to their comfortable, relaxed height. Each time you practice this, notice how much lower your shoulders are going. You may find that you have lowered them by several inches as relaxation replaces tension.
It may be helpful to set an alarm on your phone or watch to go off every few hours to remind you to check in with yourself again. Eventually, this will become a habit, and you won't need the alarm anymore. Keeping

tabs on how you are feeling will help you by giving you the opportunity to nip any adverse energy in the bud and help to restore your good health on all levels. It also helps to teach you mindfulness or being conscious of what is going on within you. There are few greater health tools than awareness of what is going on in your mind, body, and spirit. Knowing these things and addressing them right away can give you a huge leg up in your quest for contentment.

Chapter 4

FREEIMAGES.COM/INGRID MULLER /PIXABY.COM GERALT

Visualization - How to Get Around the Blind Spots

Visualizing is one of the most emphasized techniques in law of attraction programs. We are told to visualize being in the job we want, the relationship we want, the house that we want. Meditations are based on visualizing calm, peaceful sceneries, or seeing money fill your hands and your bank account. This is great if you are a visual person but not everyone is. Many struggle just to see a glimpse of these great sounding visuals but end up feeling frustrated and disappointed when they can't see the images no matter how hard they try. The good news is, is that you don't have to be visual to engage in meditations or any law of attraction program. Because I am also not naturally visual and endured many frustrating hours of trying to visualize, I realized that my innate sense of "feeling" would be just an effective tool and it is. It inspired me to create the test below for other non-visual people to help them to determine their own dominant senses to help them with an alternative to visualization. This has also helped me to become more visual and may help you to as well.

All of us were born with dominant senses which can be used in the place of visualization and are just as effective, perhaps even more so because you will be able to truly immerse yourself in them to help you achieve your goals. The first step is to figure out what your dominant sense is. The test below will help you to make that determination.

Determining Your Dominant Sense

This brief test will help you to determine what your dominant sense is. Look at these sets of phrases and make a note of those that most describes a phrase that you would use, you can choose more than one for each section. Then using the letters attached to each phrase, figure out which you chose the most and match them to the table to figure out what your custom dominant senses are.

If you are in a questioning situation

A. It doesn't smell right to me
B. It doesn't sound right to me
C. It doesn't feel right to me
D. It doesn't look right to me
E. It doesn't taste right to me
F. I don't think that's right

If questioning what another person is saying to you

A. That idea stinks
B. I feel differently than you do
C. I don't see your point
D. I'm just not hearing you
E. It leaves a bad taste in my mouth
F. I don't think you know what you are saying or talking about

When angry

A. That person's attitude reeks!
B. There was a roaring in my ears!
C. I was so hot/cold/numb
D. I saw red!
E. I wanted to hit him so bad I could taste it!
F. I thought my head was going to explode!

Table of Senses

If your answers are mostly A's then your dominant sense is smell.
If your answers are mostly B's then your dominant sense is hearing.
If your answers are mostly C's then your dominant sense is feeling.
If your answers are mostly D's then your dominant sense is sight.
If your answers are mostly E's then your dominant sense is taste.

If your answers are mostly F's then your dominant senses are your thoughts.

It is important to note that you can have more than one strong sense. It is typical to have a dominant sense and then a secondary one. For example, if you chose 3 A's and 2 D's then your dominant sense is smell and your secondary is sight.

- ✓ It doesn't smell right to me - Clairscent
- ✓ It doesn't sound right to me - Clairaudient
- ✓ It doesn't feel right to me – Clairsentient
- ✓ It doesn't look right to me – Clairvoyant
- ✓ It doesn't taste right to me – Clairgustance
- ✓ That's not how I think of it or I don't think that's right – Claircognizance

Once you have determined what your dominant senses are, you can use those in place of visualization. For example, let's say you are listening to a guided meditation about walking on the beach. Instead of visualizing the beach, if you are clairsentient, you can feel the warm sand beneath your feet and the mist of the ocean on your skin. If you are clairaudient, you can hear the crash of the waves against the shore or the sound of the breeze around you. If your dominant sense is clairgustance, you can taste the salty air around you or even the salty water of the ocean as you imagine walking in the surf. Using your own dominant sense will be much more enjoyable and much more effective than struggling to see what just isn't there.

Tips to become more visual while engaging your dominant sense

Once you determine your dominant sense, you can also use it to help to develop your other senses. You do this by first engaging your dominant sense and then try to also tap into your lesser senses such as visualization.

Exercise
Using your dominant sense to feel/taste/smell an orange. If you are clairaudient, when you peel an orange it makes a "scratch" sound as the peel pulls away from the pith and fruit. Hear that sound. Once you are

feeling/smelling/tasting/ hearing the orange, try to see it or try to tap into one of your other non-dominant senses in order to develop that gift. It can be a lot easier to visualize after first engaging your dominant sense. Once you have mastered a lesser sense, do the exercise again and add another sense you want to develop to it.

The extra added benefit to doing this is that the more you develop your other senses, the more psychically aware you can become as you embody and develop all of your senses. This will also help you to engage not just in visualization but a full sensory experience as you imagine yourself achieving your goals. This can greatly strengthen your law of attraction abilities.

Additional alternatives to visualization:

Meditate on affirmations designed to convey the outcome you are looking for instead of visualizations. It may be easier for you to repeat a phrase in your mind than to visualize a scene. Write out the words you are meditating on and keep them in front of you so that if your mind drifts, open your eyes and read from the words to literally put your affirmation in front of your eyes and bring your focus back to where it needs to be.

Use Your Imagination

You might not be able to visualize, but I bet you can imagine. Remember when you were a child and imagined being a famous ballerina or astronaut? Maybe you imagined being a fighter pilot or dreamed of what your wedding gown would look like. Even now you might imagine winning the lottery or getting that big screen TV you always wanted. Your imagination is one of the most powerful tools you possess and it's something no one can ever take from you. You can use it for guided meditations just by imagining the scene they describe as opposed to trying to visualize it. When focusing on your goal, instead of trying to visualize it, simply imagine achieving it and how wonderful that would feel.

Use a visual aid-

If you can't visualize a pile of money sitting in front of you to take as you please, go online and bring up a picture of a pile of money or gold or whatever form of currency you feel most comfortable with and gaze at it while reaffirming your intentions. Look at the picture as if it were really a pile of money in front of you and engage in the positive emotions that come along with it.

If you need to evoke feelings of peace, pull up an image of a soothing forest, mountain or ocean scene. If looking at kittens brings you joy, pull up a picture of cuddly kittens and let the feeling of joy suffuse you, then reaffirm your intentions for happiness while engaging in the true feeling of it brought on by looking at the kittens.

Does seeing your favorite sports team win bring up the feelings of excitement and achievement within you? Pull up a picture or video of them winning a game or doing their exercises to evoke that feeling within you and then mentally reaffirm your intentions of achievement for whatever goal you are trying to reach.

For prosperity, pull up a copy of your bank statement online and print it out or use the printed one you get in the mail. White out the balance and write in the balance that you want or need. Change the date to the date that you need it by and then pin it on a wall in front of you and gaze at your new balance. Let the relief or gratitude, happiness and excitement of seeing that big bank account fill you and you engage in the awesome feeling of financial security. Gaze at the date to let your subconscious know that you need the money by then and let yourself feel the joy of having all the money you need to accomplish your goals.

Pretend

Pretending is another effective way to replace visualization. Let's travel back in time again to when you were a child. Did you jump off your bed while pretending you could fly like a super hero? Did you play with your doll or teddy bear and pretend it was a precious living being that sat down to tea with you? Perhaps you threw a sheet over some chairs and pretended it was a fort that you were valiantly guarding against enemy forces. You can still use the awesome technique of pretending when doing guided visualizations or meditating on what you wish to achieve. Instead of visualizing strolling down a beautiful garden path, just pretend you are. Or, instead of visualizing sitting at the desk of your new job, sit back and pretend you are in your new office chair, happy and ready for work.

Write It Down and Read It Out Loud

Yet another way to effectively replace visualization is to sit down and write out exactly what your goals are. So instead of visualizing owning your new cherry red car, write down all of the attributes of the car you want, along with the cost of it, so you know how much money you need to attract. Then on your paper write, this car is so awesome, it has (list attributes) and let yourself get excited with anticipation as you write down all of the features of your dream car. End with something like, "I am so grateful that I will soon have my perfect car. I am so fortunate and grateful that the Universe will assist me with this". Then read the whole thing out loud. Why out loud? Because not only are your eyes seeing the words, you are also hearing them which gives you doubly strong attraction energy to help you get what you want. You are also engaging the energy of sound vibration which can also enhance your LOA techniques and results.

Daydream

I love daydreaming. As a Pisces, this comes naturally for me and I consciously allow myself daydream time every day. Surely you have daydreamed about something that would please you like finding that perfect mate or perhaps getting a new speed boat and racing through the water with the sun on your face and the wind at your back. Take some time each day to daydream about achieving your goals and how that would feel and what you will do when success is yours.

Just think

If you are not the whimsical type, then just optimistically think about what you want. Think about achieving your goal and what you will do when you do so.

These are just a few ways to help you find a positive way to attract what you want without "visualization". Once you start to consciously utilize your imagination, you will probably come up with more ways of your own.

CHAPTER 5

Understanding the Lessons the Universe has Been Trying to Teach You

I probably don't have to tell you how frustrating it is to adopt a new program, follow all the steps and still end up right back where you started. It's like walking a spiritual treadmill only you don't end up in better shape afterwards.

A big part of the reason that this happens could be because we don't take the time to figure out what it was we were supposed to learn from our trials. Life is a giant learning institution and just like in regular school, it may hold us back from graduating to the next level until we prove we have the wisdom and skills to do so. That means if you are going through what feels like serious hard times, it actually shows tremendous progress on your spiritual path. We really are here to learn and when you think about your progression from nursery school through high school, the lessons didn't get easier. They increased in difficulty with each grade. The school of life is no different. The Universe may be complimenting you on a job well done by raising you to the next and harder level to see what you can do. Understanding your lessons can help you to keep moving forward on the playing board. Now this doesn't mean that once you achieve your goals, new and worse conditions will automatically arise. What it means is that whatever may be at the end of the journey, you will be much better able to handle it because of all of the lessons you have learned and the new tools you've added to your soul's tool chest.

Trying to understand the lessons can be difficult if you just try to think about it so it's best to break it down into chunks so you can look at all of the pieces thoroughly. If you are going through more than one issue such as you constantly find yourself both broke and in bad relationships, just focus on one at a time starting with the one that is bothering you the most.

One of the best ways to start to do this is by keeping a notebook or journal. First, write out the situation and think all the way back to when it started. Then ask yourself the following questions:
- What else was going on in your life at that time?
- What do you feel triggered the situation?
- What did you dislike about this situation?
- What, if anything did you like about this situation?
- Have you been in this space before?
- What were those triggers?
- What patterns of behavior are revealed as you review the situations?
- What did you dislike about those situations (this may be what you are supposed to be learning about)?
- What if anything did you like about those situations? This may be what's luring you back in.
- How did you handle the situations in the past?
- Looking back, how would you have handled it differently?
- If your friend presented this situation to you, what would your advice be?
- What have you learned from this lesson?
- If this has happened to you in the past, what did you learn from that particular lesson?
- What steps can you take to avoid this happening again?

Feel free to get some help.

If you are having difficulty figuring out your lessons, a trained professional be it a psychologist or spiritual advisor may be better able to help you. Hypnotherapists are also subconscious behaviorists and have techniques that can help you to create new life scripts. You don't have to take this on alone, there are those out there ready and willing to help you to understand why you do the things you do and how to stop doing them.

Now that I look back upon my life and see all that I have triumphed over, I realize I had no idea I was so badass!

Acknowledge Your Strength

Once you understand the lessons, forgive yourself and accept your lessons with gratitude. And as you look back on these situations, remind yourself of how strong you are, all that you have overcome, the trials you have triumphed over and pat yourself on the back. Acknowledging the strength you demonstrated back then will remind both your conscious and subconscious that you are a warrior and even if you got knocked down, you still managed to dust off and get back up again. Congratulations on your remarkable strength, courage, and persistence.

While going through the process of discovery, take care of the adverse energies that can also keep you stuck where you don't want to be. These include:

- Removing the toxic emotional energy.
- Removing the energetic cords that may be binding you.
- Taking your energy back (yes you can!).
- Balancing the body, mind, and spirit.
- Shielding yourself from adverse energies. Shielding will be discussed in Chapter 6.

JOY SERENITY LOVE HOPE PRIDE EXCITEMENT

OUT WITH THE BAD, IN WITH THE GOOD
HOW TO RELEASE TOXIC EMOTIONAL ENERGY

Energy Cleansing Step 1

Caveat – The techniques given below do not apply to grieving over the loss of a loved one. If you are grieving over the loss of another or something that has meant a great deal to you, the grieving process will take place naturally although the techniques given may still help. If you are grieving, attending grief support groups may also help you. Being around others who understand your pain and who will support you through the grief process can help you immeasurably.

These techniques are also not meant to take the place of medical care for those who are clinically depressed or have chemical imbalances that cause emotional unrest. However, the techniques may act as a compliment to your medical treatment.

Before we can effectively communicate with our subconscious, we must first clear the air so to speak. In this section, we will address the importance of first releasing the adverse feelings that may be holding you back and tips on how to do it. As I said before, I refer to these adverse feelings as "alarm" emotions since that is what they are. They are here to warn you that something is wrong and needs to be fixed. It's breaking away from the emotion so that we can think clearly that is hard. This is also not your fault.

You may not have been told when you were growing up that emotions are also tools of discernment. Instead of recognizing that whatever is triggering our alarm needs to be examined for cause and then resolved, you can get so caught up in these adverse feelings that you can end up feeling drained and unable to see any hope in sight. Think of it this way, if you were swimming in a lake and started to feel very tired, would it be best to swim back to the shore to rest up safely on land? Or, should you just tread water until you are too exhausted to even try to make it back to the shore? The logical answer would be the former, but unfortunately, many of us choose the latter, not because we want to but because no one may have told us that alarm emotions are a tool, not an ocean that you can drown in.

In order to even begin to sustain pleasant thoughts, we must first shed ourselves of the toxic energy that comes from being immersed in alarm emotions for a prolonged period of time. This is why you have possibly tried your best to focus on feeling confident that you will receive what you wish and on the joy that will fill you when you have it in hand. But shortly thereafter or even worse during your happiness exercises, those dread feelings of poverty, heartbreak, anxiety and/or depression over your situation come flooding back and emotionally you are right back where you started.

Again, ***you are not broken*** and with a few helpful tips, we can work towards having the true feelings of peace and happiness that allow us to attract more of the same. There are several ways to achieve this.

OLD YOU

NEW ENERGETICALLY CLEAN YOU

Prep and Clean Your Vehicle

As mentioned earlier, it is very important to get energetically shored up before embarking on such a life changing journey. In the same way that you wouldn't put freshly washed clothes on top of the dirty clothes in your hamper, empty out those alarm emotions first so that you can become a fresh, clean vessel for your new and improved attitude.

This doesn't mean that you just need to do these steps once and life is great again. Think of these protocols as spiritual medicine. Depending on your custom needs, you may be able to just do them once a day or several times a week. Or, you may need to do them 3 times a day. It's all up to your custom coping skills but don't forget that baby steps are okay.

Pull Yourself Together (Literally)

We live in a multi-tasking, need it right now or as soon as possible kind of world which can up the pressure of having to complete a multitude of tasks. This can cause your energy to literally be scattered as you think of all the things that you have to do and feel the accompanying pressure that comes with it. To help you re-center, you can literally pull your energy together to rebalance and feel better quickly.

I have a video tutorial that you can watch and follow along on my YouTube Channel. Just go to **www.youtube.com** and put in my name to bring up my page.

YouTube Page: Rhonda Harris Choudhry
Playlist: Empath Training Mini Class Series
Video: How to Balance Your Energy in Less than 60 Seconds

Here are the written instructions for those who do not have access to the internet or who learn better by reading:

1. With your dominant hand, curl your pinky, ring and middle fingers into your palm like a half fist.
2. Make an "L" shape with your thumb and forefinger.
3. Place the tip of your forefinger on one side of your forehead and your thumb on the other.
4. Pull your hand about an inch away from your face

5. Raise your hand so that your fingers are about an inch higher than your head but still about an inch away from it.
6. Bring your thumb and forefinger together at the center point of your body just above the head
7. With the thumb and forefinger pressed together, say "Divine Balance, balance, balance...." And keep repeating the word balance as you slowly bring your hand down the center of your body until you get to the end of your groin.
8. Pull your hand away and relax

You may need to do it a couple of times depending on how scattered your energy is but you should feel better, more centered and calmer.

Acknowledge Your Feelings

With all that you may be going through, chances are you have every right to be upset so go ahead and look your problems straight in the eye and tell yourself it is ok to feel sad, depressed, angry and/or anxious. Emotions serve an important purpose. They let us know when things are going well and when something is amiss in our world. Physical pain is a message from the body saying something is wrong, please fix it. Sadness, anger, anxiety, etc. are our emotional alarm system and our heads should go up when their sirens go off and we should investigate the perceived danger. It's no different than if our house alarm went off in the middle of the night. You wouldn't ignore that your home or family may be in danger so why would you not afford your soul the same courtesy?

When we try to convince ourselves that everything is great and to feel positive about life without addressing and releasing adverse energy, our emotional alarms ring even louder to get our attention so that they won't be ignored. Give yourself permission to go ahead and examine your feelings. Make a list of what you are feeling and why. Addressing the situation in this way will now lead you to the next step towards releasing alarm emotions.

Validate Your Feelings

Remember when you were a kid and felt that you had been wronged and shouted, "That's not fair!"? Even though you might have been sent off to your room filled with righteous indignation, you still did something very important to your psyche; *you validated your feelings*. By saying that's not fair, you were really saying that you felt you had rights and that they were not taken into consideration and now you are angry about it.

Self-validation is so important. With so much literature telling us to be happy even when it seems our world is falling apart it is all too easy to start to feel guilty about feeling badly. By validating your feelings, you let yourself know that you are justified in feeling this way due to whatever circumstances you find yourself in. Yes, we should focus on overcoming the challenges causing that circumstance, but first, we have to release the emotions that are exacerbating it. Just by validating your feelings and asserting your natural right to experience and express them can go a long way to making you feel stronger. It reminds you that yes, your feelings do matter.

Acknowledging your feelings and then validating them can also inspire you to work harder to improve the situation and allow you to take a more objective stance to help you think clearly. It is hard to come up with resolutions when our thinking is so clouded with alarm emotions. This takes us to the third step.

Releasing the Emotion

Some people are able to release alarm emotions through exercise. They can pound a punching bag, run 5 miles or just walk, allowing each step to drain away unhealthy energies. Others can meditate their cares away, going to a spiritual place of peace and contentment. But what about those who aren't athletic and who haven't yet mastered the art of meditation? No problem, we can still fix this.

You have rightfully allowed your emotions to do their job by warning you. You have acknowledged them and validated your right to feel exactly how you are feeling. The next step is to release them by realizing that they have already done their job and no longer serve you. This also lets the Universe know that you are aware that work needs to be done and you are willing to do it. To the Universe, you have now set the intention of feeling better and resolving your challenges. You have also opened the door to allow the flow of beneficial law of attraction energy to come in and help you with this. You may find yourself being helped by supportive people or have the resolution to a problem just come to you out of the blue. Either way, you have now set a positive course for the law of attraction to help you. Here are some exercises to help release alarm emotions that anyone can do.

FREEIMAGES.COM/ALJOSA JAPUNDIZIC

Send Them into the Light

One of my favorite ways to release alarm emotions is to send them into the Divine White Light of the Sacred Source of All Well Being to be healed and resolved. Why send them into the Light? Because adverse energies can hang around even after you cast them out of your energetic field. You don't want to cast out nasty energy just to have it settle into your living room, bedroom or wherever you are where it can continue to affect you. Even if you cast it outside your home, surely you don't want it to go drift over to your neighbors to adversely affect them. By sending it into the Light, it is healed and the energy is recycled.

I have a video tutorial that you can watch and follow along on my YouTube Channel. Just go to **www.youtube.com** and put in my name to bring up my page.

Page: Rhonda Harris Choudhry
Playlist: Empath Training Mini Class Series
Video: How to Spiritually Remove Depression, Anxiety & Negativity from the Body Mind & Spirit

Here are the written instructions for those who do not have access to the internet or who learn better by reading:

- Place your hands about shoulder level, palms up and make the following statements:
- "I recognize that I am feeling (angry, sad, depressed, anxious, etc.) and I am valid in feeling this way. But this feeling does not serve me."
- Lift your palms up towards the sky and say, "So I send it into the Light to be healed and resolved as I am healed from it".
- Put palms together in prayer position and slowly bring them down the front of your body until in front of your chest while sayings, "and I restore my Divine Peace and serenity."
- Allow yourself to feel the peace that you bring down from the sacred source of White Light and let it infuse your entire being.

Get Into Your Element

Astrologically, we all have a sacred patron element that has been assigned to help us. We can use the energy of these elements to cleanse and empower us. This can be done using the physical element as well as the energy of the element. Always say thank you for their help. To physically use the elements:

If you are a Fire sign, surround yourself with candles using the color that represents purity for you. To some that may be white candles while others may choose blue. Remember, everything you do is custom to you. Sit in the center of the candles and ask the element of Fire to help you and picture, visualize, feel or imagine the flames burning away your cares and cleansing you of worries. To say thank you, sprinkle a dried rose petal with cinnamon and infuse it with your gratitude. Using a pair of tongs, hold the petal over your sink or a fire proof surface. With an extended lighter, set the petal aflame as you thank sacred element of Fire for its service. You can also burn the petals on a charcoal block in a fireproof vessel.

If you are a Water sign, simply sitting in a tub of water infused with lavender oil for peace or rose oil for nurture will help to cleanse and restore you. Use whatever scent represents the way you want to feel. Ask the element of Water to clear you of adverse energy and to send it safely down the drain. This can also be done in the shower using

70

lavender scented soap or whatever scent makes you feel peaceful. As you stand under the showerhead, allow your cares to drain away and peace to take its place. Thank the Water for her help and walk away in peace. To say thank you, turn on the spigot and take a teaspoon full of sugar and let the water wash it down the drain as you say thank you. You will probably actually feel the energy shift.

If you are an Air sign, smudging yourself with sage to cleanse you of excess negativity works wonders. You can also use any incense that makes you feel peaceful. Just light the stick of incense and use it to surround yourself with the healing energy of the sacred element of Air. If you are using a charcoal block to burn the incense, place it in a raised vessel such as a mini cast iron cauldron, set it on the floor and walk around it as you sweep the smoke up and around you. Thank the element of Air for assistance and leave feeling light as a feather. Burn lavender incense to say thank you or take a spoonful of dried lavender leaves and blow them in the direction of the East in gratitude.

If you are an Earth sign, go outside and play in the dirt. Place both hands palms down on the ground and ask the Earth to absorb the adverse energy and cleanse it for recycling. Then if possible, lay flat on the ground and allow yourself to feel the Earth energy encompassing you, centering you and bringing you peace. Just standing on the ground preferably in your bare feet will do the job. To say thank you, place a coin on the ground or offer a glass of wine or juice. Thank the Earth for her support and walk away feeling grounded and ready to be infused with positive energy. Note, if you live in an apartment, you can fill an aluminum baking pan or plastic foot soak tub with earth which you can buy at stores that sell garden supplies and stand on it instead. I have a balcony that I have spread earth over so I can stand on it and bend over and put my hands on it as well.

Bring in the energy of the elements.
If you are unable to or don't care to use the physical elements, you can achieve the same effect by using the energy of the element.

I have a video tutorial that you can watch and follow along on my YouTube Channel. Just go to **www.youtube.com** and put in my name to bring up my page.

Page: Rhonda Harris Choudhry
Playlist: Empath Training Mini Class Series
Video: How to Use the Sacred Elements to Cleanse Your Energy

Here are the written instructions for those who do not have access to the internet or who learn better by reading:

If you are a Fire sign- Imagine that fire is safely swirling around you. Feel the heat against your skin, hear the flames crackle around you as it burns the adverse energy away, always into the Light to be healed and resolved. Say thank you when done and mentally blow a kiss to the element of fire.

If you are a Water sign- Imagine that water is swirling around you. Feel the water against your skin, hear it swirling and splashing around you as it washes the adverse energy away, always into the Light to be healed and resolved. Say thank you when done and mentally blow a kiss to the element of water.

If you are an Air sign- Imagine that air is flowing around you like a tornado, blowing all of the adverse energy into the Light until you feel light and refreshed. Say thank you when done and mentally blow a kiss to the element of air.

If you are an Earth sign- Imagine that you are immersed in a warm and comfortable mud bath. Feel the mud drawing out the adverse energies and sending it into the Light. Finish by imagining a cool rinse, feeling the water over your skin as it rinses away the residue. Say thank you when done and mentally blow a kiss to the element of earth.

Let's move onto the next step which is removing the adverse energy cords that could be keeping you from realizing your goals.

Energy Cleansing Step 2

FREEIMAGES.COM/LOTUS HEAD

REMOVING THE ENERGY CORDS THAT BIND YOU
(Empaths and highly sensitive people pay close attention)

Hopefully, you've tried the self-cleansing exercises in the previous section. If you have, you've made an excellent start on clearing out the adverse energetic debris that may be keeping you tied to the challenges you've been facing. Here is the next step and one of the most *crucial steps* which is getting rid of the energy cords that people shoot into you that drain you of the energy <u>you need to succeed</u>. ***Empaths should pay particular attention to this section.***

We are all energetic beings, and we all need fresh energy to survive. You've probably heard of energy vampires who go around sucking the life out of people, but technically we are all energy vampires since we all need energetic fuel to run on. Most of us get it from our food or exercise. Sunshine, moonlight, nature walks, and meditation can also replenish our energy. So can many crystals and herbs. But there are those who do use the human energy field to fuel up on. That means your energy field particularly if you are in the following industries:

> ➢ Spiritual service
> ➢ An industry that requires you to touch people (massage therapist, reiki practitioner, reflexologist, acupuncturist, hair and/or nail artist, etc.).
> ➢ Mental and/or physical health
> ➢ Or just a highly sensitive and/or caring individual as most spiritual people are.

While there are those who consciously feed on the energy of people, most of the people who feed on your energy probably have no idea that they are doing so. Certainly they recognize that they feel so much better after speaking with you, but for the most part, they are clueless. It would be great if they walked around in black capes lined with bright red satin and displayed especially long and pointy teeth so you could identify and avoid them but alas, they look just like you and I. They are our friends, families and perhaps even our lovers and our only clue may be that we feel exceptionally tired in their presence while they perk right up in ours. Even worse, they can transfer their problems to you through that same energetic cord which can cause all kinds of problems including physical ones.

Empaths are also at high risk no matter what field they are in because they draw in the adverse energies of others like a sponge, usually unconsciously. Many people who are of service are empaths but are unaware of it. If you are unsure if you are an empath, ask yourself these questions:

> ➢ When you are around sad people, do you get sad?
> ➢ Do people, even strangers, tell you all of their problems?
> ➢ Do you feel the need to help others even if it compromises achieving your own goals?
> ➢ Have you ever helped others and their life got better, but your life got worse?
> ➢ Is it hard to be around lots of people even if it's just in the grocery store?
> ➢ Are you constantly exhausted?
> ➢ Do you suffer from lower and/or upper back and shoulder pain? (This is where we carry the weight of the world).

> ➢ Do you go to the doctor and they can't figure out what's wrong with you?

There are many more symptoms, but the above will give you the gist of it. I have always identified strongly with the Statue of Liberty. I had thought it was because she represented a strong and powerful woman, the Divine Feminine. When I realized I was an empath, I recognized that what was really drawing me were the words she carries which symbolize the attitude of many empaths:
"Give me your tired, your poor,
Your huddled masses yearning to breathe free,
The wretched refuse of your teeming shore.
Send these, the homeless, tempest-tossed to me.
I lift my lamp beside the golden door."

If you answered yes to even a few of the above questions, chances are you are an empath also known as an energy buffet. The same way the statue lifts her lamp to attract the downtrodden, you've come to Earth to help others and your Divine Light shines so brightly that you become a beacon for all of the heartbroken, the needy, the narcissists and anyone else who feels your energy can help them. At any given time you can find yourself in the midst of these people who see you as a 24 hour all you can eat energy buffet, no reservations required.

What these people are actually doing is shooting energy cords into you that allow them to transfer their alarm emotions to you while nourishing themselves on your positive energy. You may find that as people are heaping their problems onto you, their energy perks up while you feel yours draining away, the longer you are in their presence.

This is why you can help someone out and their life gets better and yours gets worse. It's because they may have effectively transferred their karma to you and their bad luck can continue to be transferred through these cords.

It gets worse. You could've helped someone 10 years ago and they may still be feeding on your energy through those same cords. It's no wonder that you may be walking around tired and confused with so many people injecting you with their adverse energy and taking your positive energy away with them. The worst offenders can actually become addicted to your energy, so they keep coming back for more and throw a fit if you try to end the relationship.

The blessings and plights of the empath are so deep that I can't cover everything here but will be in my upcoming book dedicated to helping the empath. However, I do have an entire playlist on YouTube dedicated to helping empaths and highly sensitive people to get their own energy back and learn to shield themselves from the energy of others. You can watch them here:

Page: Rhonda Harris Choudhry
Playlist: Empath Training Mini Class Series
Towards the bottom of my page you will see "Play Lists" and right beneath it, you will see Empath Training Mini Class Series. You can also check out my other playlists as well.

In the meantime, it's important that you remove these cords so you that can get your own energy back to focus on your own goals.

Also, note that you don't necessarily have to be an empath to have cords placed into you. Everyone can be vulnerable to the energetically needy, especially if it's a close friend or family member.

To get rid of these cords, we must remove them from their roots. Some suggest cutting them but cords are like weeds and can grow back. Even worse, they can reattach to the person whose energy you are trying to get rid. That's why it's best to remove them and their roots completely so you can heal and move on with your life. Of course, after you remove them it will be up to you to consistently practice shielding techniques to keep their cords off of you in the future. Shielding techniques will be covered in chapter 6.

Many of the cords that are placed in you are attached to the various chakras located in our body. Chakras are energy vortexes. Most people focus on the main 7 which are:
The crown located at the top of your head.
The 3rd eye located in the center of your forehead just above the brow.
The throat chakra located in the center of the throat.

The heart chakra located in the center of the chest.
The solar plexus located an inch or 2 above the belly button.
The groin chakra located and inch or 2 below the belly button.
The root chakra which is located at the base of the spine just above the tailbone.

There are actually many more chakras located throughout the body, but for now, we will focus on the main 7. There is so much information about chakras available that I won't go too deeply into their definition and functions but here is a chart to give you a basic idea. The important thing for you to recognize is that the energy from your chakras provides tasty treats to the energetically needy. Like slipping a straw into a cool glass of lemonade on a hot day, they slip their energetic cords into the chakra that will feed them what they need. Since you also need this energy, losing it may also cause physical ailments in the areas listed in the chart on the next page that correspond to the chakras. Please note that other healing modalities may have various definitions of what the chakras represent, their colors, etc. I am conveying what was taught to me through my reiki studies and direct channeled wisdom from the Divine. In the resource section, I have included my favorite link to understanding the chakras. But I encourage you to advance your chakra studies on your own. On the next page is a general chart to help you understand the chakras and their functions.

CHAKRA	COLOR	MAIN MEANING	BODY ORGANS	EMOTIONS
ROOT	RED	Life force energy, prosperity	Adrenal Glands, Spine, Intestines	FIGHT OR FLIGHT
GROIN	ORANGE	Creativity in all forms, including creating the type of life you want	Kidneys, Liver, Bladder, Sexual Organs	Self Esteem, Sex Drive (Physical and Emotional)
SOLAR PLEXUS	YELLOW	FORCE OF WILL	Abdominal organs and excretory organs above	Will Power and Will Flow. Control Issues
HEART	GREEN	LOVE	Lungs, heart, circulatory system	Love, Stress, Joy, Grief
THROAT	BLUE	COMMUNICATION	THYROID	Emotional Communication (yelling, crying, laughing)
3RD EYE	INDIGO	Intuition and how you see the future	Pituitary, Pineal (Melatonin, Sleep) Eyes,	Emotional Outlook
CROWN	WHITE/LAVENDER SILVER/GOLD	Spirituality, mental health, thought processes	Spirit and Brain	Spiritual Emotions (Sympathy, Empathy, Peace)

If you are suffering from physical pain or ailments, take a look at the chart to identify the chakra that rules over that area and then give extra care to that area by sending the proper color into it when doing the cord removal.

After you remove the cord, you then have to heal the hole it has left. If you have ever had an IV needle attached to your arm, once they pull the needle out it leaves a hole that has to heal. Energetic cords are very much like IV needles. When you remove an energetic cord from your system, it also leaves a hole that needs to be healed. The healing instructions are also included in the cord removal procedure below.

Due to time constraints, the instructional video only goes over the main 7 chakras, but we actually have many more including in our hands and feet. It's important to include clearing the hands because a lot of our energy flows through them, particularly through the fingertips and the palms. Having these areas blocked can give the feeling of having your hands "tied" because the blockages may have stopped the energetic flow that you need to create the life that you want.

The same holds true for the feet which are also huge energy channels. Having your feet energy blocked can give the feeling of not being able to move forward in life and can block the beneficial energies of the earth from giving you the fuel you need to power up and keep moving.

FREEIMAGES.COM/KIMBERLY

Energy Cord Removal Process (Energy Cleansing Step 2 Con't)

Here is a video tutorial to remove these cords that you can watch and follow along on my YouTube Channel. Just go to **www.youtube.com** and put in my name to bring up my page.

Page: Rhonda Harris Choudhry
Playlist: Empath Training Mini Class Series
Video: How to Remove the Cords, Karma & Burdens of Others

Here are the written instructions for those who do not have access to the internet or who learn better by reading:

1. Over each chakra, as if unhooking fish hooks from them, unhook and then hold your hands at shoulder level, palms up and say, I unhook and release the adverse cords karma and burdens of others and myself and send them into the Light to be healed and resolved as I am healed from them.

2. Place hands back over chakra and continue with, "and restore my own Divine Peace, strength, good health, free will and the optimum flow of Divine Balanced Energy. These wounds are healed as I send in Divine _____ Light."

3. Now visualize, feel or imagine the color of the chakra flowing through. Here are the chakras with a reminder of the colors.

- Crown - White, lavender, silver or gold. If you don't know what color yours is or should be, it is safe to go with white or lavender.
- 3rd - Eye Indigo
- Throat - Blue
- Heart - Green
- Solar plexus - Yellow
- Groin - Orange
- Root - Red
- Hands and Feet - White

Visualization Alternatives:

If you are not visual and find yourself having to remove cords without your trusty color chart, you can use the alternative techniques given in chapter 4.

Here are just a few of them to remember when you are out and about and need to remove cords.

See the words – Non visual people may not be able to see colors, but they usually can see words. Seeing the color as a word can be just as powerful as seeing the color itself.

Feel instead of visualizing. For those of you who are not visual, instead, imagine the color being conveyed through a colored lightbulb and just *feel* the gentle warmth of the bulb against your skin.

Just speak or think the words.
Words are also extremely powerful. They carry the vibrations of our intentions. After you place your hands over the chakra that you are working on, speak the color into the chakra either mentally or out loud. For example, just saying or thinking, "I safely send the sacred color red into my root chakra to cleanse, heal and empower it", should get the job done just fine. Be sure to first do this over all of the chakras and then if

you need to, go back and give extra color and energy to the ones that need it.

Quick Chakra Cleanse – If you don't have much time, you can do a quick cleanse by "lightbulbing" the chakras. Simply infusing them with the right colors can go a long way into healing them and correcting the damage. You still need to remove the cords, but in a pinch, this will help.

Lightbulbing your chakras before you get out of bed in the morning will help you to start the day with balanced energy. This, in turn, can help you to feel better, think more clearly and start the day with a positive, feel-good attitude that can have an uplifting effect on your whole day.

You can also do this at any point in the day when your energy is dropping or you feel unbalanced. If you are in the service industry, you can do this throughout the day as needed. This is particularly helpful for those in the service industries such as massage therapists, healthcare professionals, reiki practitioners, etc. Taking a moment to lightbulb your chakras after each client will help you maintain your energetic balance and help keep you properly fueled up for your work.

To lightbulb your chakras:

➢ Imagine a lightbulb in the appropriate color of the chakra you are working on and then imagine that it is pressed against that chakra.

➢ Next in your mind's eye, turn on the light bulb and imagine that it is filling your chakra center with beautiful light.

➢ Then either out loud or mentally say three times, "cleansing, healing, purifying, charging with the sacred color _____."

➤ Use white lightbulbs to go over arms, hands, and feet. These areas also contain chakras that can be compromised from the energy of others and the challenges of life in general. Energy that is blocked in the feet can cause you to feel stuck in one place. Energy that is blocked in the hands can cause you to feel like "your hands are tied" in various parts of your life. Again, either out loud or mentally say three times, "cleansing, healing, purifying, charging with the sacred color _____." Naturally, you can just use one hand to do the other, but you can use both hands to do both of your feet at the same time.

As promised in chapter in chapter 2, if you are an adrenaline addict and like to do energy work, you can also transmute anxiety and even depression into pure energy and infuse it with positive intentions. You might as well make it work for you instead of against you.

I have a video tutorial that you can watch and follow along on my YouTube Channel. Just go to **www.youtube.com** and put in my name to bring up my page.

YouTube Page: Rhonda Harris Choudhry
Playlist: Empath Training Mini Class Series
Video: How to Make Anxiety Work for You by Transmuting the Energy

Here are the written instructions for those who do not have access to the internet or who learn better by reading:

Before you begin, first determine where you feel the anxiety. Many feel it in their heart area or the solar plexus but it can emanate from any of the chakras or other parts of the body as well. This is where you are going to pull the energy from.

With your hands, pull the energy away from the body part being afflicted and say:
"I purify this anxiety/depression that I feel with the sacred elements of earth, air, fire and water and restore it to pure energy which I now infuse with my intention that it grant to me, bring to me, create for me, attract to me _____ (good luck, a new love, prosperity, etc.) Through positive ways and means"

Open your palms and raise them to release the energy and say:
"I send it out into the Universe for the fulfillment of my wishes."

Place hands over the area you pulled the anxiety from and say, "and restore my Divine Peace and Serenity."

Next, if you pulled the energy from a chakra, imagine the color of the chakra going into that area. If you make a withdrawal, you must balance it with a deposit. If you pulled the energy from a non-chakra body part then you can just use white light or the color that represents peace to you.

Doing maintenance to maintain your chakra health is important to your energetic state. Here is my meditation you can use on a regular basis to help keep your chakras healthy:

The Pink Lotus Realm Meditation on Blog Talk Radio

Go to Blog Talk Radio at http://www.blogtalkradio.com and enter into the search, **"Goddess Radio The Pink Lotus Realm Chakra Meditation"**. The meditation will come up for you to listen and relax to.

After healing your chakras, you can also program them as well with intentions to help keep you balanced, focused and vitalized.

I have a video tutorial that you can watch and follow along on my YouTube Channel. Just go to **www.youtube.com** and put in my name to bring up my page.

Page: Rhonda Harris Choudhry
Playlist: Empath Training Mini Class Series
Video: How to Program Your Chakras for Success

Here are the written instructions for those who do not have access to the internet or who learn better by reading:

Place your palms down over the crown of your head and mentally say, I safely heal and energize my crown chakra so that my thoughts are clear, strong and peaceful. Place your palms together in prayer position and say thank you.

Over the 3rd eye – I safely heal and energize my 3rd eye so that my intuition is clear, strong and so that my future success is secured. Place your palms together in prayer position and say thank you.

Over the throat – I safely heal and energize my throat chakra so that my communication is clear, strong and harmonious with those I am communicating with. Place your palms together in prayer position and say thank you.

Over the heart – I safely heal and energize my heart chakra so that my kind heart is safe and protected from those who take my kindness and service for granted and to protect it from being subject to the pain of the world. Place your palms together in prayer position and say thank you.

Over the solar plexus – I safely heal and energize my solar plexus so that my will is strong and my desires are manifest but in a way that retains its peace. Place your palms together in prayer position and say thank you.

Over the groin – I safely heal and energize my groin chakra so that my creation energy is strong and I can successfully create the life that I desire. Place your palms together in prayer position and say thank you.

Over the root chakra – I safely heal and energize my root chakra so that I have the safe and optimal energy to continue forward with all that I want and need to achieve, to keep me prosperous and vitalized. Place your palms together in prayer position and say thank you.

Over the feet – I safely heal and energize my feet so that they have the strength and energy to carry me forward on my path to success and positive evolution. Place your palms together in prayer position and say thank you.

Press your hands together – I safely heal and energize my hands so that they are a safe and strong conduit for the powerful energy that flows through them to help me in my works. Place your palms together in prayer position and say thank you.

Place your palms down, one on each side of your head. As you slowly bring your hands down say or think, "I send any excess energy that I do not need into the earth to be purified and recycled."

Turn your palms up and as you slowly raise them back up to your head say or think, "and restore my Divine Balanced Energy." Place your palms together in prayer position and say thank you.

Energy Cleansing Step 3

How to Call Your Purified Energy Back to You

Now that you have cleared the adverse cords and energies from your being and turned off your energy spigots, it's time to get your energy level up even higher by recalling the <u>purified</u> energy that you have given to others.

Just like our physical bodies contain our unique DNA, so do our energetic bodies. When you consider the amount of energy that you voluntarily give to others and combine that with the energy that others just take from you with their cords, it's no wonder that you may often feel drained and exhausted and rightfully so. Large chunks of your energy, energy that you need to manifest your dreams is constantly being syphoned out of you. You may feel as weak as a person who has lost a large amount of blood. The difference is that person can go to the hospital and get a blood transfusion to replenish them from a blood type that is harmonious with their own while you may be left exhausted and confused as to how to get your energy back up. You too can get an energy transfusion to replenish you and the good news is there is no need to look for a donor. The energy that you have given away and even that which has been taken from you can be recalled to you in an instant. Since this energy carries your DNA, it can assimilate right back into the body quickly and easily. All you have to do is call it home.

The important thing to remember is to only recall your *purified* energy. You certainly don't want energy that still contains the adverse energies of those you gave it to or who took it from you.

But what if I wanted to give that person my energy to help them? Isn't rude for me to just take it back? What if they really need it? No worries. The second step of the process hooks that person into the healing energy of the Divine Light. This allows the Light to take over and heal and help them while you get to have your own energy back. This way you will have the energy you need to continue your manifestation work and to allow you to still help others without compromising your own energy levels.

For example, let's say one of your friends comes to you for advice and tells you that their boyfriend has broken their heart. They can pull energy from your heart chakra because that's where they need the healing. If they say that they hate their boss because he gives them such a headache, they can be pulling energy from your crown or 3rd eye since that's where they need the energy. By putting your purified energy back into your chakras, you revitalize and heal them so that they can do their jobs more effectively. Plus you get the extra added bonus of having extra energy. You can do this technique throughout the day if you like, especially if you are in the service industry and constantly using your energy to heal and help others.

In the interest of time, the video tutorial that demonstrates this procedure shows only how to do this in general. To add to it, please practice the technique over all of your chakras as well since this is where much of the energy is drained from you.
It is also recommended that you do this technique over your hands and feet as you did with the energy cord removal.

I have a video tutorial that you can watch and follow along on my YouTube Channel. Just go to **www.youtube.com** and put in my name to bring up my page.

Page: Rhonda Harris Choudhry
Playlist: Empath Training Mini Class Series
Video: How to Take Back the Energy that You Give to Others

Here are the written instructions for those who do not have access to the internet or who learn better by reading:

How to Recall Your Purified Energy
Pointers:
➢ Always remember that you are calling your energy back through the Light to be purified before it comes back to you.
➢ Make the mental association that purified means through the Divine White Light of the Sacred Source of All Well Being. This will then make it become your intention which is important in any energy work.
➢ If you choose to use your own Deity and or color, you can substitute them with the Divine (color of your choice) Light of my sacred Deity _____.
➢ You can also use whatever terminology works with your spirituality. Remember, everything has to be custom to you.

Steps:
• Hold both arms held in front of your body, palms up.
• Bring hands towards you in a scooping position up over your crown chakra.
• As you bring hands closer to you, state: "Taking back the purified energy that is mine…"
• Push hands outwards away from your crown as you say "and leaving that of the Holy and the Divine.
• Put hands together in prayer position and say thank you. In this way, you are both taking back your energy and replacing it with Divine Energy.
• Repeat these steps over each chakra, your hands, and your feet.
• Repeat as often as you like.

You can also use this technique to recall other things that you have missed back to you such as:

- Your good health, be it physical, mental or spiritual
- Your prosperity
- Your passion for whatever (life, hobbies, fun, etc.)
- Your happiness
- Your serenity

The possibilities are limitless.

ENERGY CLEANSING Step 4

BALANCING THE
BODY MIND AND SPIRIT

The importance of balancing and simultaneously *utilizing* all three energies of the body mind and spirit cannot be over emphasized. It is one of the greatest keys to restoring and maintaining your energetic health. Each part is powerful, important and contributes to your thoughts and feelings. They are the three cylinders that you run on. Unfortunately, many people are just running on one or two energetic cylinders.

Some people are thought based and utilize much of their minds analyzing everything, daydreaming and or being introspective but may not be very physically active. Others may be very spiritual and combine that with their physical energy by taking long walks or jogs through the parks on the beaches. But that person may not be very analytical, so they aren't optimally utilizing the energy of their minds.

Keep in mind that you don't have to be using all three faculties at the same time, but you should be using *the energy* of all three at the same time, so you have that extra strength to help you to keep on going. Even if you are fortunate enough to be running on all three batteries, if you are tired and stressed out over financial issues or other life challenges chances are those batteries have run down anyway.

It is also not that uncommon to find that these three energy providers are at odds with each other. The mind may be insisting that the body start to exercise and eat right while the body ignores it and continues to sit on the couch and eat chocolate while watching television.

The spirit may be insisting that the way out of your travails is to snap out of the depression, count your blessings and petition the Universe or use other spiritual ways to obtain freedom from that which binds you. Unfortunately, the mind may be so mired in despair that it doesn't even hear the spirit calling or is just too tired and disgusted to respond.

Add to the above your job/school and family responsibilities and chores and it's easy to see how your energies can be pulled in so many directions which can leave you feeling weak. By bringing the body mind and spirit back into alignment, you will have three sources of energy to keep your energy levels up and help you to feel stronger.

I have a video tutorial that you can watch and follow along on my YouTube Channel. Just go to **www.youtube.com** and put in my name to bring up my page.

Page: Rhonda Harris Choudhry
Playlist: Empath Training Mini Class Series
Video: How to Balance the Body Mind & Spirit

Here are the written instructions for those who do not have access to the internet or who learn better by reading:

- Place hands palms up at your sides.
- Say "Body Mind and Spirit" together.
- Snap your fingers (both hands).
- Repeat the above three steps two more times.
- Say "Balance" and snap your fingers at the same time you speak the word.
- Repeat the above step two more times.

- Do this when you need an energy boost.

Congratulations! If you have completed all of the cleansing exercises, you should be feeling lighter and more energetic. Do these every day for the first week and then you can do maintenance 1 – 3 times per week depending on how you are feeling.

Keep in mind that your subconscious may put up a fight at first if it's used to you being anxious, depressed or just stressed out. Your diligence in keeping this up will eventually convince it that you are supposed to feel good and then it will help you maintain it. Chances are you didn't get into your current state overnight and you probably have more than one issue that you are trying to resolve. Give yourself permission to take the time to nurture and heal yourself even if it's only for a few minutes a day. You are worthy of the same attention that you give to others.

Get into the pleasure principle of healing –
With all the things that you have to accomplish during the day, it can be really easy to think of this as yet another chore to add to the list. Think of your self-healing time as nurture time. This is a time of peace and pleasure that you have earned so safeguard that time and take complete advantage of adding/restoring bliss in your life.

Hopefully, by now, you are starting to feel better knowing that there is absolutely nothing wrong with you. You just needed a bit of training to learn how to function with your optimized energy as opposed to limping along burdened down by so much emotional and energetic debris.

Now that you are all cleaned up, it's time to shield up.

Chapter 6

Shields Up!
How to Use Filtered Shielding to Protect You from Adverse Energies

Shielding yourself from the adverse energies around you can go a long way in helping to maintain your energetic, good hygiene. *This is even more important if you are an empath or a highly sensitive person.* Since you are often under psychic assault with everyone's emotions coming at you, it is especially important to use shielding techniques to protect yourself.

Keep in mind that even if you are not an empath and don't necessarily feel this adverse energy, it can still be affecting you. Many health ailments are silent such as high blood pressure, cancer, kidney and heart disease but can still be devastating to the body. Often by the time they are diagnosed, the ailments may have already progressed into the danger zone while you had no idea of what was happening. Adverse energies can be just as insidious and since they can weaken your energetic field, this may translate to a lower immune system due to fatigue and the other damages inflicted from being assaulted by them.

There is a lot of information on various types of shielding methods which I encourage you to research to find additional techniques that resonate with you. You can never know too many ways to protect yourself. I will go over techniques that have worked for me and other empaths that I have trained and continue to provide links to my shielding videos on my YouTube Empath Training Playlist to further assist you.

Filtered Shielding *(empaths pay close attention)*
The importance of psychic shielding cannot be over emphasized. You may have heard that to protect yourself you should surround yourself with white light or a bubble. For many that works perfectly fine but for the empath, this may not be the best choice. White light is a hard shield and empaths need a constant flow of fresh energy to help flush out the energy of others. Placing yourself in a bubble or within a sphere of white light can actually be smothering to an empath and make them even more tired than they already are. This is why it helps to use a form of filtered shielding with the intention that it lets the good energy in but blocks the adverse energy from entering and compromising your energetic field.

There are many types of filters that you can use and typically I will experiment with a bunch of them with my clients to help them find the one that's best for them. It helps to practice with a partner, but you can practice on your own and then try out the techniques when you are around other people. Don't worry about seeing them if you are not visual. Just imagine that they are there. The types of filters I commonly practice with are:

Various types of fencing:
Picket fence
Chain link fence
Wood fence
Barbed wire fence (for extreme defense)
Wrought Iron fence

Nets
Nets also work well. You can practice using with them using the different colors that represent the elements. Try these, using the one that corresponds to your element:
Water – Teal
Earth – Brown or green
Air – Yellow
Fire – Red or orange

You can also imagine that the nets are actually made from elements to give them an extra added boost.
I also practice with nets of various shades of light. My current favorite is a net of golden light. You can practice with the various shades that represent protection to you. First, determine the color that you need by asking these questions:

When you feel you are in an unsafe situation, what color represents safety to you?

If you are in the presence of people who drain you of your energy, what color represents protection to you?

If you feel like people are projecting adverse energy towards you, what color represents defense to you?

Using the colors that represent these things to you will strengthen your shield because they resonate with your inner belief system. This is better than just using someone else's definitions of safety and protection because their ideas may not resonate with yours. Remember, everything needs to be custom to you.

TIP – Nets can be used for blocking other types of adverse energies and help you to snare the beneficial energy that you want.

For prosperity – a green net with the intention that it attract and allow energies that promote your prosperity but block those that would be adverse to it.

For energy – A red net with the intention that it attracts and allows fresh energy to vitalize and restore you while blocking those that would drain and weaken you.

For good health – a white net with the intention that it attracts and allows energies that heal and promote good health on all levels of your being while blocking those adverse energies that may contribute to illness.

For love – a pink net that allows and attracts loving people who resonate with you and blocks those that are not worthy of your affection.

You can come up with your own colors and intentions to help you achieve the life you are striving for. You can also use multiple nets at one time.

You should first practice mentally placing these shields around you by yourself to get the hang of it. If you don't do a lot of energy work already, start by practicing for just a few minutes each day. Energy work can be like physical exercise and may make you tired when you first start. Also, take frequent sips of water because energy work can also be dehydrating.

Experiment with the different types above and also try to create some based on your own custom ideas on colors and types of shields. After you feel you have found the type of shielding that makes you feel the best, you can then move on to practicing with a partner.

Solo Practice
Sit comfortably in a chair and imagine that you are surrounding yourself with one of the shields above. Pay close attention to how it makes you feel.
Does it make you feel safe?
Does your energy feel more contained?
Does it make you feel peaceful?
Continue practicing with different types of filters and colors until you find the ones that work best for you. You may find that different ones work better for different circumstances. Don't worry if don't have someone to practice with because you will be able to use objects as your

partner which will be discussed more in the section of shielding over objects.

Partner Practice
Sit across from your partner and first practice sensing their energy connecting with yours. This is an excellent way to fine tune your sensing skills which can warn you right away when you are in the presence of someone projecting adverse energies so you can immediately shield up. You can also practice this through video chat with your partner as opposed to in person.

After sensing the connection, one by one, imagine placing the different types of shields outlined above between you and your partner. Make a note of how each one makes you feel. You may find that you feel no different with some while others make you feel safe and peaceful. Once you have found the ones that work best for you, allow your partner to do the same.

Once you have found the shields that work best for you, you can then start to practice on the people you encounter at work, school, the store, etc.

The Safe Space Shield
The safe space shield is typically the easiest to use and also very effective because it mentally puts you in your own personal safe space. First, determine where you feel the safest. It could be in your home, your car, your parent's house, etc. Some feel safest on the recliner in their living room while others prefer their bedroom. After you determine what place represents a feeling of safety to you, whenever you feel the need for shielding, imagine that you are in your safe space. For example, let's say your safe space is sitting at your kitchen table. If you are at work and people are projecting adverse energies at you, mentally put yourself at your kitchen table so that feeling of safety surrounds you. This is one of my favorite shields because it's easy to imagine myself in my home where I feel safe and comfortable.

Energy Protection Gloves – Psychic Protection for your hands.
Gloves also make effective shields that block energies that are adverse to you. Consider all of the things that you touch every day that others

have touched before you. The same way that we leave our physical fingerprints on objects, we also imprint our energy on them as well. When you swipe your card in the grocery store and then enter your pin on the keypad, you can become susceptible to picking up the adverse energies that others have left on it. Think of that energy as psychic germs that can infect and compromise your energetic, good health.

Shopping carts are also a carrier of these germs. If you see someone who is obviously sick with the flu, sneeze, and cough over a cart before putting it back for the next unsuspecting person, you will probably avoid that cart like the plague to avoid getting sick. Instead you may choose another cart not realizing that it too is covered in the energetic germs of others. Think of all the people that have gripped the bar of the cart with one hand while arguing with someone on the phone with the other or yelling at their children to behave. Maybe they are sad over a relationship or enraged at their boss. Either way, that energy can cling to the cart after they push it away and you can pick that energy up when you claim the cart to shop with. PS, so can your food and other items you are buying. I'll teach you how to clear your cart but first back to the gloves.

Grocery carts and pin pads are not the only culprits. If you work in an office and touch other's pens, files, desks as well as what's in the communal kitchen, you are also exposed to the energy germs of those who have also touched these things. Wearing energy gloves at work can help to lessen your exposure to the adverse energies of your coworkers.

The same way you can pick and choose filtered nets for shielding, you can do the same with energy protection gloves.
Lace
Golden net
Fishnet
Gauze
I personally like gloves of golden netting, but you can choose the type and color that works best for you. To put on your gloves, hold your hands in front of you and simply think or say, "I cover my hands in energy gloves of (color and type such as red lace) that allow safe energy that is beneficial to me in and blocks out energy that is adverse to me.

97

Thank you." You may feel a tingle in your hands as you say this. Practice with various types and colors to see which ones feel best.

These gloves will help to protect you from all of the things your touch. It helps to just put them on in the morning so that they are in place for the rest of the day.

Quick Grocery Cart Cleanse
First, determine what color represents purity to you. Then imagine that color infusing the cart with the intention that it purifies it of all adverse energies.

If you are having a hard time imagining the color, just think or speak the words, "I purify this cart on all levels of all adverse energies with the sacred color _____".

Now shield up yourself and go shopping.

Shielding Objects
Placing shields over common objects can also help to keep your energy cleaner.

Phones – Phones are energetic devices that can provide good energy or adverse energy depending on the conversation. When we receive calls with good news, we can feel the happiness of the person on the other end of the line as they share their joy with us. On the flip side, phones can provide a direct injection of adverse energy right into your own energetic field as well. Consider holding a phone against your ear while the angst-filled voice of your BFF is pouring out their woes or your frustrated boss is venting to you. All of that energy is going right into your own energetic system and compromising its safety.

Computers/tablets – Social media can be fun as we check in with our friends and family and keep up to date on what everyone is doing. It can also be a source of adverse energies as we read stories about tragedies they are facing, angry political posts and rants interspersed with stories of suffering going on in the world. These posts contain the emotions of our friends and family and whether good or bad, we can become subject to them. The same applies if you like to read the news online or get disheartening emails.

Televisions – Even if you don't watch the news, television sets are probably one of the biggest emotional energy projection devices ever made. Even though the shows you watch may be based on fiction, the actors and actresses still have to actually feel those emotions in order for the viewers to feel them as well. That means if you watch shows with sad or stressful elements to them, those emotions are being projected right into the space of the room the television is in and right into your energetic field and that of your family. Unless you only watch comedies, your television can be bringing toxic emotional energy right into your home.

How to Shield Objects –
Shielding objects takes but a moment and is very simple to do. Simply pass your hand over the object vertically, diagonally and horizontally while saying, "shielded" as you wave your hand in each direction. I call it my "shielding six ways to Sunday technique". You can also try using just one direction to see if that is adequate for you.

It's important to first feel the energy that the device is projecting so that you can feel the difference after the shielding. Take your television for example.
Start by sitting in front of your television with it on and take a moment to get a feel of the energy coming through it. For extra added effect, turn to one of the news channels where all kinds of chaos are going on. You've got commentators yelling into the mikes, a nonstop ticker of what's going on in the news scrolling constantly across the screen and reporters and guests tossing their opinions into the fray. You may be amazed at how you've watched these channels before and never noticed the harsh energy that is emanating from your television set or computer. If you are a crime documentary buff, go ahead and put one of those shows you love on but pay attention to the energy that is being projected into your room. You may find that it's not pretty.

Once you've got a feel for the energy coming through your set, pass your projective hand over the screen using just one direction and saying shielded and then wait a moment to see if you feel a difference in the energy coming from the TV. Then try the other directions one by one to determine which one feels the strongest. Next try all directions back to back while saying shielded to see if that works best for you. You can also move your hands in the direction that you feel would work best for you such as a spiral motion, a figure 8, or a rectangle that traces the outline of your screen. As always, everything should be custom to you.

Next, try the same techniques over our phone, tablet, computer, etc. to help block harmful toxic energy from entering your home.

Shielding Videos

Here are my YouTube shielding videos. Much of what was just discussed is on them, so they are mainly posted here for those who like to learn visually and audibly.

Just go to **www.youtube.com** and put in my name to bring up my page.

Page: Rhonda Harris Choudhry
Playlist: Empath Training Mini Class Series

Video 1: Empath Training How to Use Filtered Shielding

Video 2 : Filtered Shielding Over Objects

Video 3: How to Shield Yourself from the Negative Energy of Objects 2

The next step is clearing your personal space(s) of toxic energy debris.

CHAPTER 7

FREEIMAGES.COM/Antonio Jiménez Alonso

HOW TO CLEAR YOUR HOME OF TOXIC ENERGY AND ENTITIES

Now that you have blocked adverse energies from coming into your home by using your electronic devices as portals, it's time to get rid of all that stagnant, toxic debris that may be keeping you mired in energetic quicksand.

Have you ever noticed that when there are a bunch of happy people in a room, the room reflects that happiness? You can walk into it with no idea of what's going on and start smiling just from the positive energy that greets you at the door. That's because everyone is so light hearted and that energy is projected into the room and permeates it. Even after everyone leaves that energy remains as you smilingly put away dishes and clean up.

The same is true when it's a sad occasion and everyone feels heavy-hearted so the mood in the room is sad, and that miasma of adverse energy still lingers even after everyone is gone. Instead of smilingly cleaning up after your guests leave, you may feel so drained that you just leave it all for tomorrow.

101

Excess negative energy does not just have an adverse effect on you but also your whole environment. This is why it's very important to regularly clear your home and other personal spaces of accumulated adverse energy. Notice I said excess negative energy. We are like batteries and have a positive charge and a negative charge, and we should strive to maintain a balance between our positive and negative energies. You should never try to cleanse all of the negative energy out of anything because it leaves you and your space unbalanced. Can a battery work at full capacity with just its positive side working? It's when there's an excessive amount of negative energy that the problems can begin. Instead of thinking it as negative energy, think of it as toxic or adverse energy. This way when you use those words with your intentions, you make it clear that you only want that which is harming you to go.

I am going give you my technique to fully cleanse your home as well as some quick tips in case you don't have the time to do the full clearing. I also encourage you to research other ways of clearing your home because different techniques work for different people. Since many people use the internet to search out techniques, I will cover a few things that may not be pointed out in the various techniques that are posted on the web.

Furniture - Everyone has their favorite piece of furniture to sit upon. You probably have your favorite chair that you sit in at the kitchen table as does the rest of your family. The same applies to your favorite spot on the couch or the recliner that only you are allowed to sit on. The reason you feel so comfortable in the same seating is because it contains your energy which makes it a part of your comfort zone. The problems can arise when you are in a prolonged state of agitation, depression, fear, anxiety, etc. Those energies also permeate your furniture and if you don't clear it, then every time you sit in your favorite chair, you plop right back down into the toxic energy you are trying to get away from. Couples who have a fight while on their bed may not be aware that the energy of the anger they feel may be sinking right into their mattress so that even when they make up, that adverse energy can continue to cause problems.

Now that you know how to clear yourself energetically, clearing your furniture becomes even more important. If you take the time to cleanse yourself energetically and then go sit on the sofa, it's like trying to take a fresh bath in dirty bathwater and may hamper or undo all of your hard work. So make sure when you do your home clearings to include the furniture.

Here are some quick tips and tricks for those who just want to do a quickie cleanse. Below that are my full house clearing instructions that will teach you how to not just clear the home but also close portals and set up barriers within the home and the outside perimeter.

Quick Tips to spiritually cleanse your home:
Clove Oil – Adverse energies and entities clear out when the smell of clove oil fills the air. For some reason, they just hate it so using clove oil in a room will usually clear it out in no time. Place a small amount of oil on the index finger of your dominant hand and make a cross on all the walls and over the doors and windows. Then sit back and enjoy your nice clean space. This works especially well if your only problem is a buildup of toxic energy. However, if you have actual adverse entities in your home, this may be just a temporary fix. They will leave while the smell of cloves is in the room but may return once the smell goes away. Clove oil on your walls should last a few days, but once the smell of cloves goes away, you may have to do it again if the adverse energies start to rebuild. If you don't want to put oil on your walls, you can burn clove incense or boil cloves. Remember to always put your intentions for clearing and cleansing your space into whichever technique you choose.

Sage smudging – Filling the air in your home with sage smoke is an awesome way to clear it. However, it's important to put your intention in the sage by telling it what to do. Herbs have many properties. Sage represents purity, protection, wish fulfillment, etc. If you don't tell it what to do, it doesn't know what property to bring you so it may not be doing the job as effectively as you hope. Once you light it, ask that it clear your home of all adverse energy. Here is the chant I use to clear my home with sage:

"Element of air, hear my plea and remove all excess negativity, negative entities and unbalanced energies.
From corner to corner and end to end including all the walls, floors, furniture and ceilings, let peace and protection reign here-in. All energy that is adverse to me, my home and all of the inhabitants are now cast into the Light to be healed and resolved and Divine Peace and Protection take their place. Thank you."

You can use this chant to put your intentions into whatever tool you use including other elements which will be discussed below. Simply replace the element of air with the element that you are using.

Notice that I again said excess negativity. It's important to keep balanced energy in the home which means we need equal parts of both positive and negative energy to keep the peace the same way a battery has both a negative and positive charge to keep things running smoothly. By removing only the *excess* negative energy, you can keep the balance in your home instead of throwing it off kilter by trying to have only positive energy. While it may seem normal to want to only surround yourself with positive energy, the true goal is to have Divine *balanced* energy flowing through your home.

Smokeless Smudging – Some people can't be around smoke due to health problems or if they just don't like it. You can still clear and cleanse your home with smokeless smudging by boiling cinnamon and or other clearing and protective herbs. You know how when you make soup, the aroma fills the entire home making everyone question when dinner will be ready? The same way that smell of soup fills the rooms, the closets and often even outside the home if the windows are open, you can fill every nook and cranny of your home with the cleansing combination of boiling water and cinnamon or using whatever protective herbs/oils that you like. I like to use cinnamon because not only does it smell great but represents defense, prosperity and other great properties that you can also invoke to fill your home with that energy. If you don't want to use cinnamon, you can add the protective herbs of your choice. I will include resources in the back of this book to help you determine what the best choice is for you.

How much cinnamon you use will depend on how big your house is. Experiment until you find the amount that fills your home and clears your space.

I have a video tutorial that you can watch and follow along on my YouTube Channel. Just go to **www.youtube.com** and put in my name to bring up my page.

Page: Rhonda Harris Choudhry
Playlist: Spiritual Protection & Cleansings Mini Energy Classes
Video: How to Smokelessly Smudge Your Home

Cast the negativity into the Light
When you chase bad energy/entities out of your home, they can just wait outside for you to come out so they can attach themselves to you (their food) again, perhaps take up residence in your car or go to a neighbor's space and wreak havoc there. This is why it's best to add to your intentions:
"All energy that is adverse to me, my home and all of the inhabitants are now cast into the Light to be healed and resolved and Divine Peace and Protection take their place. Thank you."

Use your personal patron element –
Depending on your astrological sign, using the element that represents it is a potent way of clearing your home and space because it has been assigned to help you.

Earth – Salt represents the earth and you can place small bowls of salt around the home with the intention that it ground out the adverse energies and guard it from adverse energetic intrusions (spirits, entities, etc.).

Air – Sage, lavender, mint and pine incense all represent the element of air and can help you clear your home.

Fire – Place black candles around the home with the intention that they absorb the excess negative energies. Black is a receptive color and can soak up and burn away those energies that just need to go. Orange candles represent the Sun and fire and can also be used to defend the home. Red candles represent Mars and war so if you are up against really gnarly energy, go with the red. Just remember to put your intentions into it. You can also go with the color that represents cleansing and protection to you.

Note: Burning a black and red candle together works very well because the black candle will absorb burn away the adverse energies and the red will defend the home. Just be sure to empower them with your intentions. You can do this simply by putting your hands around the candle and speaking your intentions. But, first take a moment to clear the candle of any adverse energies. You don't know who may have touched it before you or what kind of mood they were in.

Water – Spraying water mixed with salt and or protective oils such as clove, frankincense, myrrh, etc. over the walls and furniture can also clear it of negative energy. You can also add a little pine or lemon scented cleaner or actual pine oil and or lemon juice. You do want to be careful about spraying furniture because oils can stain. You don't actually have to add anything to the water because straight up water also works just fine as long as you fill it with your intentions to cleanse and clear your home. If you have hard water, use distilled water so that you don't get hard water stains on your furniture or other items.

For those of you with serious issues going on in the house, I strongly suggest you do a full on clearing. It helps to do this once a month regardless of the severity to help keep your home clean and clear.

Full House Clearing Instructions
NOTE: Please read the full instructions first before beginning. You should also determine what your dominant sense is first which you can do in chapter 4.

Suggested Tools
To Direct Energy:
Athame
Scissors
Sharp Knife
Forefinger of dominant hand

To Cleanse:
Earth or salt
Air (incense or herbs)
Fire (candle or lighter
Water
These can be physical or spiritual

To command
Your Voice
Your Thoughts

Sustenance
Drinking water/sports drink – Doing energy work can dehydrate you quickly so make sure you have water with you to drink. Take frequent sips as you cleanse your home.

Food – Energy work can also make you very hungry and this hunger can come on suddenly. Have fresh fruit or a healthy snack prepared in case you suddenly get very hungry while clearing your home. This will allow you to grab a quick snack and then finish your work.

Why do we need to spiritually cleanse our homes?

You've heard the expression that you are what you eat. Along those same lines, your house is what the inhabitants feel and project. This means if you had a bad day and came home in a bad mood, that energy can adversely affect the energy of the home. Have you ever been around someone who is in a bad mood and then you find that you get into a bad mood just being around that person? Everything is made of energy including the objects in your home and just like you can pick up someone else's toxic energy and have it adversely affect you, the same applies to the objects in your home. It also applies to anyone else who lives in or frequents your home.

The importance of clearing your furniture (again).
Everyone has their favorite piece of furniture to sit upon. You probably have your favorite chair that you sit in at the kitchen table as does the rest of your family. The same applies to your favorite spot on the couch or the recliner that only you are allowed to sit on. The reason you feel so

comfortable in the same seating is because it contains your energy which makes it a part of your comfort zone. The very first time you sat in it and relaxed, it absorbed that energy. Each time you sat in it afterwards, it continued to absorb your own relaxing energy, actually being programmed with it so that now when you sit in it, relaxation surrounds you. This is not so much because of the chair but because it is filled with your own energy which makes you feel comfortable sitting in it. You may find this also to be true when the family gathers, each always going to a certain spot, the one that contains most of their own energy, the energy they feel comfortable with.

The problems can come in when you are in a prolonged state of agitation, depression, fear, anxiety, etc. Those energies also permeate your furniture and if you don't clear it, then every time you sit in your favorite chair, you plop right back down into the negative energy you are trying to get away from.

What if there is an entity or spirit that's in the home?

Figure out if this is a pleasant or unpleasant being. There are plenty of spirits that just pass through or belonged to the home before you got there and mean no harm. It may also be someone you knew that passed on and has come over for a visit. If this is a pleasant energy, then it is up to you if you want to allow it to stay. If it is unpleasant, then it needs to leave. The same way that you would not allow some stranger to come in and take over your home, unwanted spirits and/or entities are to be treated in the exact same way. Kick them out.

There are a lot of programs and movies that depict horrible spirits and entities taking over homes and terrorizing the occupants. It becomes so awful that outside help is requested to cleanse the home. While there is little doubt that these homes have been taken over by unwanted spiritual guests, it is the fear of the inhabitants that enable them to stay there and grow in power.

Think of these entities as the bullies you knew in grade school. They picked on the people that they thought would not fight back and fed themselves on their victim's terror and pain. The kids that showed the most fear were the ones that were picked on the most. The children that refused to be intimidated were left alone. Show them you are not afraid and they will lose interest in you since you are essentially now starving them.

Signs that something is wrong in your home

The regular cleansing of your home can greatly help to avoid visits by unwanted beings, but sometimes they can slip through the cracks and get in. It is important to recognize the signs. Here are some.

- ✓ You feel areas in your home that very cold in comparison to the rest of the house, or your entire house is freezing or way too hot and your heating/cooling equipment is working just fine.
- ✓ You walk into your home or a room and feel irritated or angry for no reason.
- ✓ There's an odd smell, such as perfume or cologne that you don't wear or a bad smell and you can't figure out where it is coming from.
- ✓ You hear strange sounds or voices like your name being called and you can't identify the voice.
- ✓ There's a lot more fighting amongst the people in your home for no real reason.
- ✓ There's a heaviness in the home or a room
- ✓ You walk into your home or a room and become afraid for no apparent reason.
- ✓ You feel watched even when you are the only one home.
- ✓ You are suddenly inundated with bad luck and illness.
- ✓ Your pets are acting antsy and/or hiding around the house or refuse to come inside or go outside.
- ✓ You just feel like something is wrong.

Any and all of the above are signs that there may be strange energy lurking within your home.

Handling it yourself
If you are the type of person that has no problem with being aggressive against those who would try to take over your home or personal space, you can use the following to spiritually cleanse your home. If you do have a problem with being aggressive, remember that unwanted spiritual

guests are no different than a stranger coming into your home and helping themselves to whatever is yours. Would you not aggressively defend your home and family to the best of your abilities should some stranger break into your home? When you are clearing your house, adapt the same attitude that you would if it were a thief or other type of no-goodnick breaking in to cause you harm. **This is your turf, and you have the right to aggressively defend it**.

If you are absolutely too fearful to do it yourself, then, by all means, hire a reputable person to do it for you. Interview them and ask them what their techniques are. After you read this section, you will have the knowledge you need to ask them questions to verify their ability to clear your home. You may also find someone that is able to clear it from a distance. I have done many distance clearings on spiritually infected homes with success so it can absolutely be done. Visit my website if you would like to contact me to set up a consultation.

Start in the room furthest from the front door. The purpose of this is to drive the adverse energy/entity forward until you drive them out of your home. Don't forget that some of these energies are sentient beings and know exactly what you are doing so they will go and hide in another room with the intentions of coming right back out when you're done. Once you reinforce the barriers of the rooms you clear, they can't go back to them, so they are forced to keep moving forward if they are trying to avoid you. Once you reach the front room by the front door, you can cast them out of your home entirely. There are instructions included to clear your yard as well in case they decide to go hang out there. Please note that you do not have to open a door or window to cast them out. Since they are energetic beings, they can move through walls, ceilings, and other physical barriers just fine.

Kitchens, Bathrooms, Vents and Mirrors in General

Kitchens and bathrooms hold stronger fascinations for entities because they travel through mirrors and plumbing. They also like to cruise through ventilation systems. Mirrors, in particular, can become portals turning the mirror in your bathroom into a spiritual train station with passengers arriving and departing regularly. Sometimes people who cleanse homes forget to shut down the mirrors, drains and ventilation systems which can leave the door open for more unwanted visitors to slip through. There's no point in clearing the home but leaving the entryways open to allow more unwanted visitors into your home. Follow the directions below to turn these entrances into exits only. We don't want them to be able to enter, but we do want them to be able to leave. Include these techniques as you travel through each room that has a mirror/plumbing/ventilation system.

Mirrors

Hold your hand over the mirror to scan for energies like a breeze coming from it or heat penetrating the area. Press your athame or sharp knife against the edge of the mirror while avoiding your reflection to be seen in it and state, "this mirror is now an exit only. None can enter they can only leave, so it is. Re-scan the mirror to see the energy has changed. It may have been warm when you first scanned it but is now cold after you shut it. How you translate the energy will be determined by your own custom sense. Note, you can't always be totally out of the reflection of the mirror so stand as much to the side of it as possible. This is because if an entity is present and knows you are about to shut down the door to its home, it may rush for the mirror to escape and you don't want it brushing up against you on its way out.

Drains/plumbing

Press your athame against the drain, toilet, sink, etc. and state "this drain and all of its accompanying plumbing are now exits only. None can enter they can only leave, so it is. Note, this also includes washer dryers, hot water heater, furnaces, refrigerators that have water and or ice makers/dispensers. Anything in your home that water flows through.

Ventilation System

Press your athame against the vent and state, " This ventilation system is now an exit only. None can enter they can only leave, so it is.

Steps to Clearing the Home
Here are the steps to clearing your home. The detailed instructions on how to do this will follow.

1. Cleanse yourself of negative unbalanced energy, (you can use a smudge).   Doing this in an adverse state of mind may just send more adverse energy into the home.
2. Remove the toxic energy and spirits by sending the energy into the Light.
3. Close the portals and cleanse the space.
4. Put up the barriers.
5. Bring in Divine White Light from the Sacred Source of all Well Being and fill the room with it.
6. Secure the perimeters.
7. Do a room test – After cleansing the first room, stand inside of it for a moment and get the feel of it. Next, walk into another part of the house and as you do so, feel the difference. Do the uncleansed rooms feel heavier? Can
you feel residual emotions like anxiety or fear? Then go back to the room you cleaned and notice how much lighter it feels, how much crisper the air is.

This is to train you to start to notice the energetic differences in rooms. This way when you walk into a room that needs to be cleared, you will know it right away and can nip it in the bud before it gets out of control. Just remember, it's always best to clear the entire home even if just one room seems out of control. This way the energies can't just go hide in another room and infect that room as well.

After clearing the home, re-cleanse your own energy to remove any adverse debris.

Empowering your tools and elements-
Each of your tools including the elements that you are using needs to be empowered to do your bidding. Assemble the following:
A sharp pointed object
A zip lock bag of salt
A sage smudge or other protective type incense
A spray bottle of water. Note, I live in a state with hard water, so I use distilled water to avoid hard water stains.
Tea light candles or you can use big 7 day candles if you like. I like to anoint them with clove and lavender oil for peace and protection.

Athame

Start by holding your athame or sharp object in both hands feeling the energy flow and simply state, " I charge you to do my bidding and drive the adverse energy in this home into the Light to be healed and resolved." Note you can also use your forefinger, but there will be no need to empower it. You can also use a fork, a pen, anything with a tapered and preferably sharp tip.

Earth

Stick the point of your energy direction device (athame or whatever you are using) into the salt and say:
*Element of Earth hear my plea
Remove all excess negativity, negative entities, and unbalanced energies
From corner to corner and end to end
Including all of the floors walls furniture and ceilings
Let peace and protection reign here-in. Thank you.

Air

Place the point of your energy direction device against the edge of the burning incense and say the above substituting Air for Earth.
*Element of Air hear my plea
Remove all excess negativity, negative entities, and unbalanced energies
From corner to corner and end to end
Including all of the floors walls furniture and ceilings
Let peace and protection reign here-in. Thank you.

Fire

As you clean each room, when you get to the element of Fire, light the candle. Place the point of your energy direction device against the edge of the lit candle and say:
*Element of Fire hear my plea
Remove all excess negativity, negative entities, and unbalanced energies
From corner to corner and end to end
Including all of the floors walls furniture and ceilings
Let peace and protection reign here-in. Thank you.

Water

Place the point of your energy device against the edge of the water bottle and state:
*Element of Water hear my plea
Remove all excess negativity, negative entities, and unbalanced energies
From corner to corner and end to end
Including all of the floors walls furniture and ceilings
Let peace and protection reign here-in. Thank you.

Spirit/Entity Removal

Before ordering spirits out of your home, it is important to reemphasize why you must not just send it away but send it into the Light. By simply ordering something out of your home, it can jump from room to room, or go outside and perhaps sit in your car and wait for you there. It can leave and go wreak havoc on your neighbor's home or it might even try to counter attack. Ordering it into the Light bans it from coming back into contact with you or others.

Begin at the back of the home to drive any spirits forward. These techniques are to be used for each room. To order the spirit/entity out of your home, hold your energy direction device in your dominant hand. Hold your arm up over your head and begin rotating it in a circular motion and address the room in a loud, aggressive tone as though ordering a burglar out of your house:

"Hear me all that inhabit this space! Unless you are here by my invitation or you are of the Most Holy and the Divine and with Divine intentions, it is time for you to leave! I cast you into the light, GET OUT!!!!!"
As you yell, "get out", forcefully push your arm into a straight line, directing the energy upward out of your home and into the Light. Hold it there for a moment. If you are energetically sensitive, you will be able to feel the shift of energy in the room."

Bring in the Elements

Earth
Beginning on one side of the door to the room and moving around the room from that point, throw small amounts of salt against the walls, repeating the salt empowerment phrase:
*Element of Earth hear my plea
Remove all excess negativity, negative entities, and unbalanced energies
From corner to corner and end to end
Including all of the floors walls furniture and ceilings
Let peace and protection reign here-in.
Note: it doesn't matter if you move around the room clockwise or counterclockwise but make an entire circuit of the room.

Air
Beginning on one side of the door to the room and moving around the room from that point, wave the incense in a flicking motion around the walls, repeating the air empowerment phrase:
*Element of Air hear my plea
Remove all excess negativity, negative entities, and unbalanced energies
From corner to corner and end to end
Including all of the floors walls furniture and ceilings
Let peace and protection reign here-in. Thank you.
Note: If you are using a smudge or incense stick and you have carpeting, hold a small plate underneath it as you wave it around. With smudge sticks, I use a saucer, and with my fingers on the bottom of the saucer, I use my thumb to secure the smudge stick to the saucer. This helps in preventing any burning ashes that may fall from burning your carpet.

Water
Beginning on one side of the door to the room and moving around the room from that point, lightly spray water over the walls, repeating the water empowerment phrase:
*Element of Water hear my plea
Remove all excess negativity, negative entities, and unbalanced energies
From corner to corner and end to end
Including all of the floors walls furniture and ceilings
Let peace and protection reign here-in. Thank you.

Note: be careful not to spray electronic equipment or anything that can be harmed by getting wet. When you go over those areas, just hold the bottle up and imagine that the area is being washed in water energetically.

Fire

Place your candle in a safe spot in the room. Light it and repeat the phrase, Element of Fire hear my plea
Remove all excess negativity, negative entities, and unbalanced energies
From corner to corner and end to end
Including all of the floors walls furniture and ceilings
Let peace and protection reign here-in. Thank you. It will continue doing its job as it burns since you have empowered it.

Putting Up the Barriers

Placing protective barriers within the walls of the room helps to ensure that no other adverse influences can enter. This is done by injecting the energy of earth, air, fire and water collectively in each wall to form a powerful and protective energetic force to protect each room. Here is where knowing what your dominant sense is comes in handy since this is an energy projection exercise using that sense. The effects are so much stronger if you can engage them by seeing, feeling, tasting, etc. based upon your own dominant psychic senses. If you have not yet done so, please visit chapter 4 and take the test to see what your dominant sense is.

If your dominant sense is feeling, then you can *feel* the elements going into the walls, the rush of air, the heat of fire, etc. If your dominant sense is taste, then taste the element of earth as you send it into the wall or if it is hearing then hear the crackle of flames as you inject the energy of fire into the wall, etc.
This technique can also come in handy if you need to clear a space and you don't have the physical elements handy to clear the outer part of the room. Instead of spraying water against the wall, you can use your dominant sense while imagining the room is filled with water and is being washed of all of the adverse energies. Or instead of physical smudging, you can use your dominant sense to imagine a tornado swirling in the room and dispelling the adverse energies.

Note, if you are unable to use your dominant sense to raise the energy of the element to project it into the walls you can also write the name of the element onto the wall with the forefinger and press it into the walls with your hands.

Also be aware that putting up barriers does not mean that this barrier will hold forever. It needs to be maintained and reinforced each month when you do your house clearing. If enough people bang on and push against a locked door, eventually that door is going to give. This is why it's important to try to do this on a regular basis. If you can't do it once a month then at least try to do it at the first sign of energetic disturbance in the home in order to maintain a peaceful space.

Instructions for putting up barriers: Place your palms against the wall or if unable to do that, use your mind to direct the energy. Use these instructions for all of the rooms in the home. You are not just putting the elements into the walls, you are also putting your own energy into them to mark your territory.

NOTE: If your spirituality associates different directions with the elements, you can adjust these instructions to suit your own direction/element belief.

Air
Consider the spiraling energy of a tornado, how it can destroy anything in its path and blow gigantic objects out of the way as though they were feathers. This same force can be put inside your walls for protection. Place both hands against the wall and use your dominant sense to bring up the element and press it into the wall.
Picture, visualize, feel or imagine air swirling in the wall.
State: Element of Air I charge thee to fill and protect this space from adverse unbalanced energies and entities. So it is. Thank you.

Fire
Consider the protection a wall of flames can bring you, burning away those pesky adverse energies. Place both hands against the wall and use your dominant sense to bring up the element and press it into the wall.
Picture, visualize, feel or imagine fire swirling in the wall.

State: Element of Fire I charge thee to fill and protect this space from adverse unbalanced energies and entities. So it is. Thank you.

Water

Consider the force of a tidal wave, how it washes everything in its path out of its way. Place both hands against the wall and use your dominant sense to bring up the energy of the element and press it into the wall.
Picture, visualize, feel or imagine water swirling in the wall.
State: Element of Water I charge thee to fill and protect this space from adverse unbalanced energies and entities. So it is. Thank you.

Earth

Consider that earth can ground out fire and electricity. In the same way Earth has the ability to ground out dangerous energy, it can help to keep your home safe by grounding out the adverse energies so that they no longer exists. Place both hands against the wall and use your dominant sense to conjure up the element and press it into the wall.
Picture, visualize, feel or imagine earth swirling in the wall.
State: Element of Earth I charge thee to fill and protect this space from adverse unbalanced energies and entities. So it is. Thank you.

All of the Elements

If you have a lot of experience doing energy work, you can also use all of the elements at once, visualizing them filling the walls by stating, "Element of Earth , Element of Air, Element of Fire, Element of Water, protect this space, protect this space, protect this space!" Say this while pressing your hands against the wall and do all walls in the room and home. If you don't have a lot of experience with energy work, then add the elements to the walls individually.

NOTE: If you live in an apartment and have people above and or below you, also do the floors and ceilings to block whatever adverse energies their apartments may contain.

Bring in Divine White Light from the Sacred Source of All Well Being and Fill the Room

Finish each room cleansing by filling it with protective peaceful spiritual energy. Holding your energy direction device in both hands above your

head point it at the ceiling and then rotate your hands so that the point points down to the ground as you state: I now bring down the Divine White Light from the Sacred Source of All Well Being and fill this room with peace and protection always. So it is. Thank you.
Don't forget to do the room test!

Outdoor Perimeters for Houses

The same way it is important to shore up the barriers inside your home, protecting the perimeters of the home and yard, in the same way, will help to keep unwanted influences out of your yard. You can use the above steps to secure the perimeters of the home.

First, clear the space. I have found it best to clear the space first before putting up the barriers. This way you are securing your clean space as opposed to space filled with adverse energies. Also note that although we are calling upon the Moon and stars, you can do this at any time of the day or night since the *energy* of these celestial beings is always available. You can also call upon the Deity of your choice.

Stand in the center of your front or back yard and state, "We call upon thee our Divine Brother Sun, you of the Divine Masculine, of strength and protection to fill this yard with your awesome energy, clearing all adverse energies from this yard and sending them into the Light to be healed and resolved and thank you."

We call upon thee our Divine Sister Moon, you of the Divine Feminine of healing and nurture to fill this space with your awesome light and healing, nurturing energies and fill this yard with Divine Peace and Serenity and thank you.

We call upon thee the billions and trillions of stars that fill the sky with your awesome twinkling lights of joy and wonder to fill this yard with the joy and happiness that your twinkling energy brings and thank you.

And now the Sunlight retracts and thank you. And now the Moonlight retracts and thank you. And now the Starlight retracts and thank you and I ask that you leave the healing, nurturing, strengthening and happy energies in this yard so it stays filled with Divine Peace and Protection, Serenity and Joy always, thank you. "

As you follow the instructions below, face each of the four directions in turn and use the chants to secure your properties perimeters.

Air (East)

All hail our Lords and Ladies of the East our Brothers and Sisters, Our Brother and Patron the Sacred Element of Air, Namaste (bow) Divine Honor Love Joy Peace and Respect to thee. I charge thee please cause a barrier of protection through all the boundaries that face your direction. From corner to corner and end to end let peace and protection reign here-in. Thank you. (bow)

Fire (South)

All hail our Lords and Ladies of the South our Brothers and Sisters, Our Brother and Patron the Sacred Element of Fire, Namaste (bow) Divine Honor Love Joy Peace and Respect to thee. I charge thee please cause a barrier of protection through all the boundaries that face your direction. From corner to corner and end to end let peace and protection reign here-in. Thank you. (bow)

Water (West)

All hail our Lords and Ladies of the West our Brothers and Sisters, Our Sister and Patron the Sacred Element of Water, Namaste (bow) Divine Honor Love Joy Peace and Respect to thee. I charge thee please cause a barrier of protection through all the boundaries that face your direction. From corner to corner and end to end let peace and protection reign here-in. Thank you. (bow)

Earth (North)

All hail our Lords and Ladies of the North our Brothers and Sisters, Our Sister and Patron the Sacred Element of Earth, Namaste (bow) Divine Honor Love Joy Peace and Respect to thee. I charge thee please cause a barrier of protection through all the boundaries that face your direction. From corner to corner and end to end let peace and protection reign here-in. Thank you. (bow)

CHAPTER 8

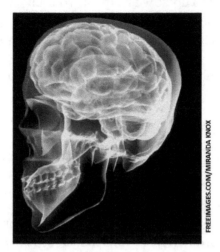

FREEIMAGES.COM/MIRANDA KNOX

HOW THE SUBCONSCIOUS MIND WORKS

We've done the prerequisite clean ups and now we are ready to get to work on our retraining our subconscious mind. As much as we would like to believe that we are in control of what we do, as previously stated the conscious mind rules only 12% of our actions. It's the subconscious that mainly runs the show and it can do so with an iron fist. It's unfortunate that the conscious part of the mind takes the brunt of the blame for our lives. Here are some things to remember about the subconscious.

The subconscious:
•Rules 88 percent of your mind and your actions
•Only understands what it feels is normal
•Is dedicated to keeping what it defines as normal in your life
•Does not like change
•Will fight to keep you from trying to break free of your "normal" boundaries
•Thinks it is giving you the perfect life
•Works from the standpoint of identification, association, and response
•Needs to be trained in the language of emotions

Most of the above list has already been covered in previous sections. What we are going to do now is expand your understanding of the subconscious so that you understand what you are up against and why you have been so challenged with manifesting your goals.

So how does the subconscious make its decisions on how to run your life?
Through:
> Identification
> Association and
> Response

The subconscious uses identification, association, and response to make decisions, be they positive or negative. These factors are largely based on your past. Unfortunately, the subconscious is not very innovative and relies heavily on how you've made decisions in the past to make decisions for your current situations. It will look at a current situation then search its memory banks to find a similar situation and then view what your response was at that time. Since it does not like change, it can cause you to make the same decision that you did back then, whether it was good for you or bad for you. It will also take into consideration the training that you received as a child. Remember, it doesn't know the difference between good and bad. It only knows what's normal and will draw on past responses and training to make current decisions.

Here are different types of training and associations that your subconscious has probably used.

Common Training and Associations That Affect the Subconscious

<u>**Gender Training:**</u> Please note that all people are not raised the same way, nor are they affected by the same things. This section discusses the general way that many were raised and how that has affected their subconscious behaviorism. Also note that despite how sexist this type of training appears to be, it was created for good reason.

Prior to 1920, there was no such thing as a teenager. You were a child until you hit puberty and then you were an adult. In 1619, the age of consent to marry was 12 for girls and 14 for boys. Even though most didn't marry until they were in their 20's, this was mainly due to it taking an extremely long time for a couple to work and save up enough to have their own home. Still, work they did to prepare for their marriages. The average lifespan even in 1900 was only 46 for men and 48 for women. Preparation for life had to begin early because it ended so early. It wasn't until life spans started to increase that people wanted children to have a longer childhood experience, so the term teenager was invented. Therefore before the invention of the "teenager" there was good reason to start training girls for marriage and motherhood early. Men as the breadwinners and protectors also had to be trained early. Times were tough and the men had to be tougher if they were to keep themselves and their family alive and healthy. This also explains why teens are so rebellious. For at the very minimum of centuries, perhaps thousands of years, they began their lives as adults at puberty. It is their inherent instinct to continue this tradition, so they demand adult rights even though they are considered children, think they know everything and want the right to live their lives as they see fit. 100 years has not been enough time for this instinct to go away. Ptolemy XIII was an Egyptian pharaoh and brother of Cleopatra, who began his reign at the ripe old age of 11 or 12. King Tut began his reign at 9 or 10. Mary Queen of Scots began her time at the throne at 16 when she married and briefly reigned as Queen of France before returning to Scotland to rule as Queen there. She ruled over two separate nations before the age of 18. Teenagers are much more capable than we give them credit for and it is understandable why they demand to be treated as adults while we still see them as children.

Things have greatly changed since then, but still, the training has remained largely the same and can play a huge role in a person's subconscious behaviorism.

Women – Historically women have been trained to be nurturing caregivers to ready them for marriage and motherhood, pretty much from the time they are born. They are given dolls that really seem to drink their bottles and actually soil their diapers, to love and nurture and pretend that they are their own offspring. They have tea parties with them, play house with them and develop a loving relationship with inanimate objects. As they coo and talk to their baby dolls, they imagine the doll responding to them with the words and warmth they want to hear and feel and they cuddle and love their dolls as if they were real living beings. These loving relationship with inanimate objects can easily set women up to have relationships with emotionally unavailable men (like inanimate dolls) and to project onto that man the responses and emotions they are hoping for in much the same way they did when interacting with their dolls.

There are also many messages about body image being thrown at them while they are extremely young and impressionable. Many are encouraged to play "dress up" and are given fake makeup kits which can send the message that their natural looks aren't good enough. This is reinforced as they watch their mothers primp in front of the mirror, mascara, and lipstick in hand. They are given plastic high heeled shoes with rhinestones and feathers attached and princess costumes with tiaras and garish fake jewelry which can be viewed as the preludes to the high heels and lingerie that adults wear. Even many cartoons that are geared for girls feature scantily clad heroines with slim waists, large breasts and big hair and makeup. This can implant the idea that you have to be slim and gorgeous in order to be strong and successful. Add it all up, and you can get a young woman who feels she needs makeup, high heels, a slim body with big boobs and fancy lingerie in order to feel pretty and who may also find themselves wondering why they always seem to be in relationships with emotionally unavailable partners. I used to love when my mother would let me play in her makeup and jewelry, spritz myself with her perfume and hobble around in her heels. This caused my own association of beauty with makeup, high heels, jewelry and pretty lingerie. Of course, I don't blame the moms out there because they have only been following the examples that were given to them either at home and or through print and broadcast media. Keep in mind that it's not that long ago that women were not encouraged to work outside of the home and the only aspirations they could have were to get married and have children which is why they have been trained to focus on marriage and motherhood as young girls, as well as looking attractive to help attract a good husband. I am grateful to see that now there is a much needed and increasing awareness of the pressure being put on women to look perfect and that the movement of promoting positive body image is growing. There are so many dolls now that promote strength, business success and various careers and body acceptance and it does my heart good. Still, these enlightened parents still have to compete with the images being projected through televisions shows, cartoons, advertisements, etc. When taking all of that into account, you can see that that combination forms a formidable army to go up against. Hopefully as time goes on, awareness will increase and alleviate all of this, but for now, some subconscious retraining may be necessary to remove the energy of these adverse influences and the effects they are having on your life.

Men – Men are typically trained differently. From the time they can walk and maybe even before, they are handed footballs, baseballs, soccer balls or toys that represent whatever sport the family enjoys. They are put on sports teams and taught how to strategize, to fearlessly face their opponents, knock out the competition and to win the game. They are taught teamwork and the value of brotherhood. They are given soldiers and or action figures to create mock wars and defeat their enemies. Many are not allowed to cry and are told that crying is for girls and that they should suck it up and be a man even when they are young boys. Telling a little boy to stop crying and act like a "big boy" or "be a man" can cause subconscious training that associates being emotionally repressed with manhood and normalcy. These trainings can teach them to be emotionally unavailable in relationships, to be loyal to their "bros" and to be aggressive in life in order to be successful. These are not bad things but can hamper relationships due to what may appear to be indifference to their partner's emotions when it is actually subconscious behaviorism that was ingrained in them very early on. This is also a part of programming designed for back in the days when young boys were raised to defend the home and provide for their families.

Empath Subconscious Training - Empaths are born with the need to help others. It is an intrinsic part of their nature. To add to this, many empaths were raised or heavily influenced by narcissists. The narcissist will train the empath child to subvert their own needs for the sake of the narcissist. The two become an imperfectly perfect pair because the narcissist is all about himself and the empath becomes all about the narcissist. Since empaths are already born to be of service, this boot camp style training from narcissists can create a lifelong struggle for the empath to focus on their own needs instead of everyone else's.

Associations

<u>Songs</u> – Hearing certain songs can invoke memories of people, places, good times, bad times or sad times and bring on the same emotions that you felt the first time it made an impact on you. How many times have you driven in your car and had an old song come on that you loved and danced to as a teenager? You may find yourself thinking of old times as you sing and dance along to the music. You might also have heard an old love song that reminded you of your first love and felt a tug on your heart as you thought about that person from so long ago. When that song began playing, your subconscious identified it as a song from your past, associated with people, places or things and then evoked the same emotional response you had back when you listened to it in the past.

While reminiscing can be fun, using past events to make current decisions can be devastating. For example, let's say you've been in a challenging relationship for some time now. Perhaps it's abusive or maybe the love is gone and you want to be free and single again. You've come to the conclusion that the best thing for you to do is to end the relationship and move on with your life. You turn on the radio, happy to have finally made this decision and a song that you and your partner used to slow dance to comes on. The subconscious steps in and identifies the song, associates it with you and your partner in happy times and brings up in you that same loving feeling that you had when you fell in love with them in the first place. Now your new decision to be free may go right out the window, and you may fall back into your same routine and remain in an unfulfilling relationship.

<u>Smells</u>- Certain smells can also invoke memories such as the scent of a certain perfume or aftershave or certain foods like popcorn popping. The smell of roasting turkey can bring back associations of past holiday dinners with friends and family. The whiff of someone's perfume may remind you of the perfume your grandmother wore as she read you bedtime stories. For that moment that you smelled that perfume, pleasant memories may come flooding back of the bonding time you spent with your grandmother.

<u>Sights</u> - Seeing an old car that reminded you of the one your family had when you were a child can bring back memories of fun road trips, battling with your siblings over the window seats and happiness from the positive expectations you hope realize at the end of the trip. Here is one of my favorite examples as told to me during my hypnotherapy training by the Hypnosis Motivation Institute. While I can't remember which instructor told the story, it stays so strongly in my mind because I can completely identify with the love of chocolate cake.

One day a man got together with one of his buddies for lunch. He was extremely proud of himself, having just lost 25 pounds thanks to a strict diet and exercise plan and couldn't wait to show off. He's silently smug as he watches his still overweight friend order a cheeseburger with fries while he orders a large salad and broiled steak for himself. He begins telling his friend about how hard he has worked to take off the weight and how determined he is to continue with this regimen to improve his health. Suddenly the waiter approaches the table pushing the desert cart. The man barely glances at it, knowing that he has the will power to refuse any of the fattening treats. That is until his eyes glimpsed a large slice of three layer chocolate cake. When he was a child, every year for his birthday his mother threw him a big party and made him a three layer chocolate birthday cake. All of his friends would come and he would get tons of presents before chowing down on the delicious cake his mom made for him. Before the man knows what happened, he's suddenly looking down at the few crumbs left on the empty plate that had once held the piece of chocolate cake. As he wipes the remnants of frosting from his mouth, he can't believe how quickly he folded and scarfed down the cake despite all of his will power. It wasn't his fault. His subconscious identified and associated that piece of cake with the cakes from his childhood birthday parties and caused the man to respond based on this past association. His diet was doomed the second he saw the cake.

Tastes – Just like the man in the story who saw the cake and threw his diet out of the window, tastes can do the same thing. Every time you eat your favorite candy, you are not just living in the moment. There is a part of you that remembers the first time you tasted one, how the sweetness filled your mouth, how smooth it was going down. Then further memories of trick or treating, the fun that went with getting your favorite candy. Seeing a box of Cracker Jacks in the grocery store may remind you of how you used to love hunting through it with your fingers to find the prize inside and that memory may inspire your subconscious to make you buy a box for old time's sake.

How the subconscious determines what is normal -
To be fair, the subconscious does not just accept any behavior as normal. You have to work at it. Earlier we talked about pleasant associations. The same holds true for unpleasant associations which lead to our bad habits. Let's use smoking as an example. In today's society, the horrible effects of smoking have been well explained, you can no longer smoke in bars, restaurants, and certain public spaces and rightfully so. But back in the olden days before people knew how dangerous it was, smoking was considered cool. Movies were full of cowboys rolling their own and smoking in the saddle. You'd see glamorous actresses taking long, languid pulls on their cigarettes and blowing out long plumes of smoke while batting their eyelashes at their love interests. Children being the impressionable beings that they are would see this and want to emulate those actors and actresses. They would sneak their parent's cigarettes and bring them to school to sneak smokes in the school yard. It was seen as the cool thing to do so many of us (me included) who wanted to be in the "cool" crowd took up smoking to do so.

Becoming a habitual smoker is not an easy thing to do and your subconscious does put up a fight at first when you introduce new and unhealthy habits. Here's how it goes.

Smoking – The first time you smoked, you probably:
- ✓ Coughed half to death
- ✓ Got nauseous
- ✓ Felt like a bomb went off in your chest
- ✓ Had the worst taste in your mouth
- ✓ Smelled bad
- ✓ Got a headache
- ✓ Got dizzy
- ✓ Did it for the coolness factor

Your subconscious said, "hey, this is awful! Let's not do this!" and tried to stop you. You may not have even wanted to continue smoking but to be cool like your friends, you continued anyway.

As time went on, you began associating smoking with
- ✓ Socializing
- ✓ De-stressing when under pressure
- ✓ Talking on the phone
- ✓ Working (believe it or not you used to be able to smoke at your desk at work)
- ✓ Drinking alcohol
- ✓ Drinking coffee
- ✓ Driving
- ✓ Or having a smoke after you eat

So finally the subconscious says, "this must be normal because you keep doing it so fine, we will continue to roll with it." Then one day after hearing all of the reports that smoking causes cancer and wreaks general havoc with your health, the health of your family and anyone in range of your second-hand smoke, it finally hits home and you sit up and take notice. You get tired of your hair smelling like smoke, your clothes and home smelling like smoke and your car smelling like a flat out ashtray. You finally decide to quit and as soon as you make that decision, conflict begins.

1. The conscious mind submits to its analytical department that it's time to quit smoking.

2. The critical mind analyzes all the data it has received and agrees. "Yes", it says. "We need to quit smoking. It's making us sick, it's expensive, it smells bad." It sends its recommendation to the subconscious for final approval.

3. The subconscious says, "What are you talking about? If we quit smoking, how are we going to de-stress? We can't talk on the phone or socialize without one plus remember how cool we felt when we were hanging out with our friends back in the day? Let's not forget the coolness factor so no, we will not quit." The decision to quit has now been vetoed.

This is why no matter how much a person wants and needs to quit, they may find the challenge too strong to overcome and can't stop which then adds feelings of failure and stupidity and just makes matters worse. When a person finally quits for a while, and diligently follows the program and ignores the cries of the subconscious to return to smoking, the subconscious will finally say ok, you're right. Not smoking is normal, so it's better that we don't smoke. But be warned. Because of your past association with smoking, it can also be easy to get addicted again even if you just have one cigarette. The subconscious remembers and can use that memory of smoking being normal to once again become the current association. In Chapter 9, we are going to learn how to use the memory association of the subconscious to help us move forward on our journey to success.

The smoking principle applies to many other types of negative "normal" behavior.

Worrying too much – We often follow the example set by our parents. If your parent was a worrier over everything or a specific thing, this can create the tendency to worry in you. Most of the things we worry about never come to pass, still, the tendency to worry is very strong in many people and it effectively ruins their life by depriving them of peace.

Poverty mentality - If you grew up poor, your subconscious can accept this as a normal state and can keep you from making money.

Relationships – If you grew up without a positive example of relationships then there is an excellent chance that you will try to recreate that situation in your own life so you can either fix it or just because that is your subconscious' idea of love.

Martyr complex -If you grew up as a caretaker, perhaps caring for a younger sibling or a sick parent, you may spend your life constantly looking for people to take care of or save instead of yourself because your subconscious recognizes this as normal. Also, as a caretaker, you may have had to put your own needs last because the priorities of the person you were caring for had to come first to ensure their safety and survival. This can train your subconscious to put your needs at the bottom of the priority list if it even lets you on the list at all. Now you spend your time putting out fires for everyone else while your personal life continues to go up in flames.

Environmental factors –
Chaos - If you had a chaotic household with lots of fighting and crises, your subconscious may try to recreate that for you because it thinks that's what life is supposed to be like.

If you lived in a household with infidelity, then either you may hook up with partners that cheat or you cheat yourself.

If you grew up with domestic violence then chances are your subconscious will recreate that for you because that is what it thinks that love is.

Communicating with the subconscious through the language of emotions
So how do we have a sit down with our subconscious to explain the way things really need to be in our lives in a way that it understands? You do so with the language of emotions. When you were a child, you used your emotions for what they were for, to understand what is good and what is bad in your life. When things were good, you laughed and cooed happily in your crib. When you were uncomfortable because your diaper was wet, you yelled and cried. These actions helped your parents to know when you were at peace or when you were sounding the alarm so that they would come running. Your emotions were your only means to communicate, so you operated on a "feeling level".

When a child is born, it is already operating on survival instincts and quickly recognizes who is responsible for caring for them. That means they have a stake in how their parents are feeling since their survival may depend on it. They pay attention and begin to understand the emotional language their parents or providers are speaking to them and then try to mirror it back to them.

When a mother sings to a baby, the baby cannot understand the words, but he does understand the feeling of loving emotions his mother is sending him. It works the same way if the mother is angry and tense, the baby will feel it. Because our subconscious training begins during our early childhood development, most of that training was given through the language of emotions. As an adult, you still speak and understand the

131

language of emotions. If someone is glaring at you, they don't need to say anything for you to feel their anger at you, or their love for you if they are looking at you in a loving way.

As the child grows older, it also begins to take its cues on what to expect in life by not just feeling what their parents are feeling but also by incorporating the spoken language with it. Now there are words to back up those feelings. As an example, many years ago I was over at a friend's house, and we were chatting in her kitchen. Her three-year-old daughter was close by playing on the floor with her toys. My friend was very upset over her and her husband's financial situation and was expressing to me how badly they needed money and how tired she was of not having any. All of a sudden her daughter began crying. We asked what was wrong and through her sobs, she cried, "We don't have any money!"

Now a three-year-old child has little concept about what money is. All she knew was that mommy was upset over this money thing, so she was upset too. Unfortunately, her parent's finances did not much improve especially since they had five children and my friend was a stay at home mom. Because they had so many young children, the cost of the daycare that would have allowed her to work was too exorbitant, so they had to make do on just the salary of her husband. This reinforced the subconscious messages of "lack" to her daughter which in turn reinforced her focus on money and getting it. Through what she was taught as a child, she felt that money must provide happiness since her mother was so sad without it and therefore to achieve happiness for her and her mom, she must acquire money.

This little girl started working when she was just 14 at a fast food place. She worked 30 hours a week and made assistant manager before she finished attending high school where she did well enough to receive a full-ride college scholarship. She is still driven to amass a fortune now that she is in her early 20's. She's made quips about how money doesn't disappoint you and is determined to be rich. This is a prime example of how the subconscious training she received as a child has influenced her entire young life, and much of that training was communicated to her emotionally.

Of course, not everyone who grows up in financially limited circumstances becomes obsessed with becoming rich. There are also those who often find themselves in dire straits just like their parents did. It all depends on the person, the environment and their own custom makeup and coping skills. Either way, the emotional communication we received as children plays a huge role in our subconscious behaviorism as adults.

This may also be one of the reasons your affirmations don't seem to sink in and take hold. Affirmations are often used to help drive a point home to the subconscious through repetition of certain phrases. This can certainly help, but it takes a lot of repetitions to finally convince the subconscious to accept the affirmations as truth and then change its behavior. Again, this is because the written and spoken language is not its primary language, emotions are. Communicating with your subconscious through your emotions can really go a long way in helping it to understand the "new normal" you are trying to create in your life and then make the changes necessary to achieve it.

Now that you understand the role your emotions play in your life, let's take another look at the surefire LOA blocker:

Self Induced Bad Karma Through Negative Self Talk
We touched on this a bit in chapter 2, but it was important to first convey a deeper understanding of how your emotions, associations, and responses affect your life before going further with the topic.

When you hear how a person may have hurt another, there's a part of you that may want that person to be punished for their bad behavior. Punishment for bad behavior is something that has probably been instilled in your subconscious since you were a child. When you did something wrong, your parents punished you. If you did something bad in school, the teachers gave you detention or called your parents to let them dole out the punishment. When you watched TV shows and saw the bad guy get trundled off to the hoosegow, you were glad because they were going to get the punishment they deserved. Subconscious translation: Bad behavior deserves punishment.

Negative self talk can be likened to you reprimanding yourself for perceived bad behavior. This can trigger the subconscious belief that that you have done something wrong and therefore deserve to be punished for it. Many are unaware of how much negative self talk runs through their heads, or they don't take it very seriously. How many times have you berated yourself for a mistake? Did you say "how could I be so stupid?" Or, "I can't believe I just did that, I'm such an idiot!" Here are some more examples:

"I look disgusting in this dress, I'm so fat!"

"I know I need to quit smoking/ lose weight/get out of a destructive relationship, but I just can't seem to do it. What is wrong with me? I'm so sick of myself!"

Did you forget to do a task and remember while in bed and say something like, "I can't believe I forgot to do that! How could I forget something so important! What is wrong with me?"

"Why am I so weak/dumb/self destructive?

"I hate my wrinkles/gray hair! I look so old!" Note how you are also directing hatred at yourself.

Calling yourself names and mentally beating yourself up can wreak havoc when trying to manifest good things in your life. Not only are you sending a signal to your subconscious that punishment is warranted but also you are adding conflicted energy into your works, but this can be remedied.

It's not that easy to just stop negative self talk, but you can get into the habit of countering it with a positive post script. While you are working on decreasing these episodes, when these damaging words do crop up in your mind add the phrases like, "but I am still awesome", smile and give yourself a hug. The very act of smiling can send positive energy through your system and counter the adverse ones and wrapping your arms around yourself for a few moments can give you the physical feeling of love and support.

Examples:

"I can't believe how badly I screwed that up, but I am still awesome." Smile and give yourself a hug.

"I'm so fat, I can't stand how I look anymore! Thank goodness I'm so awesome anyway." Smile and give yourself a hug.

"I know I need to quit smoking/ lose weight/get out of a destructive relationship, but I just can't seem to do it. What is wrong with me? I'm so sick of myself! At least I know that I am also a wonderful, caring person who deserves more so I am going to keep striving to give myself the good life I deserve." Smile and give yourself a hug.

I have a YouTube video that speaks about this and offers experiential exercises to understand how these words affect your energy. Just go to **www.youtube.com** and put in my name to bring up my page.

Page: Rhonda Harris Choudhry
Playlist: Empath Training Mini Class Series
Video: How to Make Negative Self Talk Work for You

Before we begin the training exercises, we have one more really quick clearing to do. It's important that first we stop the mind chatter that is constantly babbling away in our mind and distracting you from doing your manifestation work.

FREEIMAGES.COM MAGDA

Mind Chatter and How to Stop It

We've blamed much of our challenges on our subconscious, but the conscious mind can work against us as well. Have you ever tried to have a conversation with someone who didn't listen to anything you said and instead just kept talking over you? This pretty much sums up mind chatter. It's that non-stop voice in your head that is constantly reminding you of what you didn't do, what you have to do, what was wrong with what you did do and that you're just not doing enough. It is the right hand of the subconscious and can keep you in a state of agitation. This is particularly true if your "normal" state of being is that of being agitated. Don't forget the subconscious tries to keep things normal, so it will feed the conscious mind all the triggers you respond to.

The same is true if your normal state is one of happiness. You know those people you see in the grocery store shopping by themselves and just smiling away as though enjoying a private joke? People whose normal state of being is happiness enjoy pleasant and peaceful thoughts as the mind chatter reminds them of how awesome life is, how peace is the path to love and happiness and how lucky they are to be able to breathe, live and enjoy the miracles that occur every day. Unfortunately, this is not the case for many of us.

Being able to focus is a large component of law of attraction systems. You have to focus on your desire and the outcome you hope to achieve. Meditation is a great way to help us to do that, but if you are subject to constant mind chatter that you can't seem to turn off, then meditation may seem virtually impossible.
Here is a likely scenario:

You (trying to relax and meditate) With each breath I relax my body, I relax my mind and am conscious of the peace within me.
Your mind: Excuse me but did you pick up the dry cleaning? Also, I don't know if you noticed, but we're just about out of milk. Oh and don't forget to buy the snacks for the school trip tomorrow. What kind are you going to buy?
You: I breathe in peace, I breathe out all things adverse to me and send them into the Light. I am one with serenity (breathing deeply)
Your conscious mind: Did you schedule the tune up for the car? Did you send out those emails requesting the information you need for the staff meeting at the end of the week? Speaking of which, what else is on the agenda? You also need to make an appointment with the vet to get the dog groomed and you might want to make an appointment to get your hair done as well. The greys are getting out of control...

When you consider how much both your conscious and subconscious minds have been wreaking havoc with your intention manifestation, is it any wonder your LOA programs have not worked?

Before you begin the subconscious retraining techniques, it's best to first quiet down the mind chatter. Sitting still, breathing and counting the breaths is one way to help you relax and quiet the mind. It is also helpful to start your program techniques within 30 minutes of waking before the mind chatter starts ramping up or within 30 minutes before going to sleep when the relaxation process has already begun on its own. I also have a quick technique that you may find helpful as well.

I have a video tutorial that you can watch and follow along on my YouTube Channel. Just go to **www.youtube.com** and put in my name to bring up my page.

Page: Rhonda Harris Choudhry
Playlist: Empath Training Mini Class Series
Video: How to Stop Mind Chatter for Divine Peace of Mind

Here are the written instructions for those who do not have access to the internet or who learn better by reading:

How to Stop Mind Chatter for Divine Peace of Mind

- Hold hands over head with just the tips of the middle fingers touching, palms down.
- Say or think, I request and accept Divine peace of mind from Earth to Sky, (flip palms up)
- And from Sky to Earth (flip palms down)
- Place hands in prayer position and say thank you.
- Do this twice and the mind chatter should quiet down. You can repeat it whenever your conscious mind tries to chime back in.

Now, let's go have a chat with your subconscious mind.

CHAPTER 9

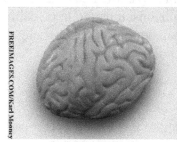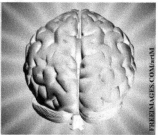

OLD CONFLICTED   NEW CLEAR &RETRAINED
MIND   MIND

RETRAINING THE MIND AND EMOTIONAL
SHAPESHIFTING

The exercises in this chapter are to help you to not only get your subconscious to work with you in a positive way, they may also help the conscious mind as well. Your conscious mind may only be responsible for about 12% of your actions, but it still can do much to torpedo your best efforts to manifest positive change in your life. This can be particularly true if you have a problem with suspension of disbelief. This term is usually used to describe the techniques used in written fiction and movies to get the mind to accept fiction as truth to better experience the suspense and/or other sentiments the story is trying to convey. I find this term also fits for those of us who may not be able to get the mind to accept what it refuses to see as anything but a lie. These exercises will also be the basis for learning emotional shapeshifting which will be discussed more later on in this section.

Our conscious mind does our critical thinking for us and depending on how strongly you can manipulate your belief system, it can put the kibosh on your suspension of disbelief. As stated before, one of the pieces to succeeding with the law of attraction is believing that you have already acquired what you are trying to manifest. Some people have no problem doing this like actors who can assume a role and believe it to the point that they appear to actually become it. Alas, other people may be analytical thinkers and not be able to convince themselves of what is not actually true. I'm one of those people. I may be a whimsical Pisces, but my Moon sign is Capricorn which is the equivalent of having Lt. Joe Friday in my brain saying, "just the facts ma'am, just the facts." Your Moon sign represents how you think. We touched on this a bit in chapter 2 where we discussed how your subconscious might be calling your conscious mind a liar. The same can apply to your conscious mind that may also be calling you a flat out liar.

Here's an actual example.

Me: I already have the $3000 I need to pay off my credit cards.
Mind: No you don't
Me: In order for the law of attraction to work I have to believe that the manifestation has already happened.
Mind: How can you believe that something has happened already when it hasn't already happened? Do you even hear yourself?

It went on in this vein for a while as I was trying to believe that I already had what I wanted. My mind won and I gave up trying to believe the untrue. Needless to say, when you are conflicted so is the energy you are putting into your intentions so before giving up my attempts at believing a falsity, all I accomplished was sending out conflicted energy that did nothing to draw me closer to my goals. Conflicted energy is a sure way to doom your results.

In the next section are exercises that will begin the emotional shapeshifting lessons. You will be pulling on emotions of the past and changing the wording to reflect the future. This way the conscious mind won't call you a liar and the subconscious will understand you better because you are speaking its language. You also get to experience an emotion based on fact instead of fantasy since it's from a real memory. Don't forget that the subconscious uses the past anyway to make decisions so by practicing these exercises you will be working within its own already established modality instead of trying to introduce new concepts that it may not understand.

Emotional Shape Shifting

**HOW TO USE YOUR EMOTIONS
TO SHAPESHIFT FROM THIS ⟹ TO THIS**

Exercise 1 - Emotional Shapeshifting
Using the Old to Establish the New

Remember when I mentioned that if a person quits smoking for a while and has just one cigarette, the subconscious can cause the addiction to reoccur because it still remembers your old associations with cigarettes and uses those memories to recreate the "smoking is normal" syndrome? This proves that you can use an old association of wealth, love, good health, etc. and with a little work, get the subconscious to accept it as normal. Depending on what it is you want to achieve, you can ride the emotions of the past to change the present and create the future you want.

Our emotions greatly influence our state of mind *and* communicate with the subconscious for us. Don't forget that in order to utilize the law of attraction, we have to feel the emotion that represents what we are trying to achieve. This can call for some serious emotional shapeshifting if you're feeling the sting of poverty or loneliness while trying to feel the opposite. More than likely, you probably already shapeshift on a regular basis without realizing it. For example, when you go to work, you probably put on your "work hat" and no matter what you may be going through in your personal life, you smile and assume the air of professionalism as you go about your work day. Actors shapeshift on a regular basis to embody the character they are playing. There are also music artists who shapeshift into another persona that represents the personality they display on stage, but that may not be a part of their offstage life. In this chapter, you will learn how to emotionally shapeshift so that you can embody the emotions you need to get what you want.

The reason I used the illustration of a caterpillar and butterfly is because many of us try so hard to become the butterfly with all of the beauty and freedom that comes with it. Butterflies can glide over fields of flowers and pick and choose the most appealing ones and then feast to their heart's content. Alas, many of us feel more like the caterpillar slogging along a leaf or a blade of grass hoping to find sustenance while not getting stepped on or eaten up by circling predators. It's time to change those alarm emotions you've been experiencing into motivation to achieve your goals

The trick is to emotionally shapeshift into what it would feel like to be the butterfly to attract the energies you need to actually become one. The way to do this is to bring up a memory that made you feel that way and immerse yourself in that memory and the feelings that come with it so that you radiate that energy to attract what you want. We all have different responses to different things. Some people may feel elated once they achieve their goals while others may feel relieved. Therefore the first thing you need to determine is what your custom response to reaching your goal will be so you know which emotion to pull on.

Step 1 – How would it feel?
Before we begin, we need to figure how we will feel when we attain what we want. Think of your goal and how it would feel to achieve it. What emotion does that inspire? Do you feel:

Content
Relief
Prosperous
Healthy
Sexy
Joyful
Invigorated
Relaxed/Calm
Loved
Courage
Hope

Satisfaction
Excited
Limitless
New Beginnings
Strong
Powerful
Happy

Below I will give examples using common themes and also add in tricks
to use if you are not able to pull up an applicable memory. I'm giving
different scenarios so that you have plenty to choose from. Although
many may have the same key words, not every statement is going to
resonate with you but at least some of the scenarios should. Since this is
a custom program, just choose the one(s) that resonate with you and
disregard the rest. The purpose of this exercise is to re-engage the
feelings of these memories to:

> ➢ Let the subconscious know in its own language what it is you
>   want.
> ➢ Remind the subconscious that we already have experienced
>   these feelings so it can use them to create a new template of what
>   is "normal" for you based on these old feelings.
> ➢ Bring up the proper emotions/feelings required to work within
>   your present LOA system.
> ➢ Bring up the feelings/emotions that are applicable to your desire
>   to combine with the other LOA techniques that will be described
>   in this and the additional chapters to really amp up your efforts
>   and your results.

After each statement will be key words describing the emotions so that
you can pick and choose a scenario that will bring up the required
emotion when launching your intentions. This way whenever you feel
the alarm emotions coming on, you can counter them immediately with
these ready memories and happy emotions to help keep your LOA
frequency running more smoothly.

Please note that this is only the first step in the custom system you are
creating for yourself. The more you practice bringing up the positive

emotions applicable to your desires, the more readily you will be able to do so when adding on the additional steps to manifest your goals.

Let's get started. Read the following statements and pick the one(s) that brings up the most positive feelings.

1. When I have a full tank of gas, I feel like I can drive to China.

2. When I see my bank balance after my paycheck is deposited, for a moment I feel wealthy/financially secure/relieved.

3. When I come home and see my children/family, I feel so much love and joy.

3b. When I see my children/family come in the door, I feel so much love and joy.

4. When I can finally climb into bed after a long hard day, I feel so relieved and glad to lie down and rest.

5. I love when the house is quiet and empty and I can finally have some peace.

6. I love when I am having a party and my house is full of people. It brings me such joy.

7. I love being outside in nature. It relaxes or invigorates me.

8. I love being snuggled up with a warm blanket and a good book that makes me lose myself in another world.

9. When I was a child, I ran and played with my friends all day and was full of youthful energy.

10. When I wear my favorite dress/suit/perfume/cologne/shoes/tie, I feel sexy/attractive/confident.

11. After a hard day, I feel so relieved when I finally get home.

12. Having my dog/cat/pet greet me at the door when I get home makes me feel so loved, missed, appreciated and grateful for their presence in my life.

13. I love to exercise! It makes me feel sexy/energized/flexible/youthful/happy/less stressed/calm/relieved.

If you were able to bring up even just a few of these positive feelings by connecting with these scenarios, then you already have the basics of the emotional language you need to communicate with the subconscious when practicing your law of attraction system. Instead of trying to visualize or imagine a hoped for scenario as already manifested, you can bring up real emotions from the past to inject into your intention setting.

Let's go over each of the above statements so you understand the emotions they are conveying and how these emotions can help you by pulling up the proper energy frequency needed to manifest your intentions. The key words are bolded so that you can easily choose the scenario that evokes the desired emotion. Feel free to add your own keywords because again, this program is custom to you.

Statement 1 - When I have a full tank of gas, I feel like I can drive to China. Even though you may inwardly weep when you pay for a full tank of gas when you get in the car and see the needle pointing to full, the feeling that you could drive across the world and back can arise within you. It symbolizes a new beginning, brings relief in knowing you've got the gas you need to get all of at least your local travels done. It can also bring up gratitude that you had the money to pay for the gas. If you can bring up that feeling of limitlessness when you are setting your intentions, that emotion alone will do much to bolster your results. **Key Words: limitlessness, relief, gratitude, new beginnings**

Statement 2 - When I see my bank balance after my paycheck is deposited, for a moment I feel wealthy/financially secure/relieved. Whether it's through direct deposit, a paper check or cash, receiving your paycheck can bring up a feeling of financial security. Even if it's going right out the door to pay bills, for that moment, you may have felt prosperous. Relief may also flood your being because now you can take care of some financial matters. There's also an underlying feeling of achievement. Every time you receive a paycheck, you reap a harvest of sorts by getting paid for your hard work. This is also the feeling you can use when practicing your law of attraction systems. Part of LOA calls for setting your intentions (planting the seeds) to manifest what you want (harvesting from those seeds). This is a feeling you can bring up and immerse yourself in it and then set your intentions for wealth and financial security.

Key Words: optimistic, wealthy, prosperous, relieved, financially secure, happy, rewarded, appreciated, achievement

Statement 3a and b – (a) When I come home and see my children/family, I feel so much love and joy (b) When I see my children/family come in the door, I feel so much love and joy. There are few greater feelings of relief than coming home from a hard day's work and seeing all is well with your family. Seeing everyone home safe and sound, engaging with them and just being in their presence can evoke feelings of warmth and love and joy within you. Even if it's just one family member, in particular, seeing them can make your whole day. It's a feeling of belonging, of connecting, of loving and being loved. If you are trying to attract a more fulfilling relationship, these are the types of feelings you want to bring up to inject into your intention work.

Key Words: loved, appreciated, gratitude, nurtured, relieved, relaxed, safe, secure, joy, connected, fulfilled

Statement 4 - When I can finally climb into bed after a long hard day, I feel so relieved and glad to lie down and rest. After a long hard day, lying down in a warm bed and letting your head sink into the pillows as you drift off to sleep can be blissful. Even though sleep is a necessity, it is also a reward. You've completed your tasks for the day and now you can finally rest. That peaceful feeling just before you drift off to sleep is the feeling you want to bring up when you want to meditate but are having a hard time relaxing.

Keywords: comfortable, peaceful, relaxed, blissful, glad, relieved, carefree, accomplished, rewarded

Statement 5 - I love when the house is quiet and empty and I can finally have some peace. Not everyone wants to be wealthy. Some people just want to have less stress and more peace. If your intention is to bring more peace into your life then that feeling that you get when you are finally alone is the feeling to bring up when setting your intentions for peace. It's also a time of freedom so that you can work on the things you want to do instead of focusing on tasks for others. You can get down to what makes you happy be it coloring in a book, catch up on your favorite TV shows, taking a nap, doing your own homework for school, etc.

Keywords: quiet, inner peace, self-focus, freedom, calm, grateful, happy, optimistic

Statement 6 – I love when I am having a party and my house is full of people. It brings me such joy. Do you just love to entertain and be surrounded by smiling people having a great time? Do you enjoy prepping for the party, dressing the tables, cooking delicious food and presenting beverages that are sure to please your guests? Do you love having everyone tell you what a great time they had and what an awesome host you are? This is great energy to immerse in for a variety beneficial shape shifts. When you are feeling lonely and doing manifestation work to bring good people into your life, shifting into the memory of being surrounded by smiling and friendly people can be just the emotion you need to vitalize your intentions. If you have to do prep work to help you get further ahead such as beefing up your resume or doing research to prepare for an important interview, bring up the joy you feel when creating tasty appetizers that are sure to please your guests. Then, shift it to joy in doing the work that will please prospective employers. This will help put you in the proper emotional state to make the law of attraction work for you.

Keywords: joy, appreciated, social, invigorated, optimistic, prepared, creative

Statement 7 - I love being outside in nature. It relaxes or invigorates me.

Communing with nature is a beautiful thing. For some, it's a relaxing and spiritually uplifting to be surrounded by trees or hear the sound of ocean waves or just lie on the ground and look at the pictures the clouds make. For others it's invigorating. The brisk air and the energizing sun all join to wipe out any fatigue and get the juices flowing again. These are the people that can go on a 10 mile hike and get more energized with each step, breathing in fresh air and leaving their cares behind them.

Keywords: blissful, energized, serene, spiritually uplifted, invigorated, relaxed, joyful, renewed

Statement 8 - I love being snuggled up with a warm blanket and a good book that makes me lose myself in another world. It can feel so wonderful to be snuggled down with a good work of fiction. More importantly, it opens you up to fantasy. Even though you know the contents of the book aren't real, still you are able to engage in the story no matter how fantastic it may seem. Fantasies can be used well in with the law of attraction. It also makes you open to possibilities which are an awesome gift to have. This scenario may be particularly helpful with those who are trying to write a book themselves. Imagining that your readers will feel the same way you do when you read a book is a great way to launch your intention for a best seller.
Keywords: open to possibilities, comfort, happy, imaginative, stimulated, peaceful

Statement 9 - When I was a child, I ran and played with my friends all day and was full of youthful energy. Remember the good old days when you rode your bike till the sun went down or played hide and seek, handball, kickball, tag, etc. till your mom called you into the house for dinner? Engage in that memory and feel that physical energy return to you. This is the perfect scenario to engage in when launching an exercise/weight loss program. Feeling that energy return to you and then do your squats, walk your treadmill or engage in whatever exercise you choose with the energy and lightheartedness of a child. You can also engage in this memory if you need energy for anything that you are trying to do.
Keywords: energized, happy, carefree, lighthearted, healthy, fit, social, limitless, strong, youthful, active, fit

Statement 10 - When I wear my favorite dress/suit/perfume/cologne/shoes/tie, I feel sexy/attractive/confident. What makes you feel sexy, attractive and confident? Is it your red lipstick or your pink stilettos? Is it your new mascara that gives you flirty long eyelashes or the new color of your hair? Perhaps it's your blue pinstriped power suit that fits you to a tee and makes the ladies give you a second look or your favorite tie or the manly scented body wash you love. If you are working on finding love, feeling more confident and

/or attractive then these are the keywords for you. Can't remember a time when you felt great as an adult? Go back into your memory banks to when you were a child. Remember a time when you felt that you looked great. It could be whenever you got to wear your favorite dress when you were 6 or your first suit that made you feel like a grown man when you were 9 or whatever age you were. If you are trying to improve your appearance, bring up that memory to keep you feeling sexy and attractive throughout the day. When we feel attractive, it shows in our energy and aura which then can trickle down to our physical looks, and after a while, you may look in the mirror and see radiant beauty projected from your body, mind, and spirit.

Keywords: sexy, attractive, alluring, confident, flirty, beautiful, magnetic, seductive, sensuous, arousing, inviting

Statement 11 - After a hard day, I feel so relieved when I finally get home. Relief is such a wonderful feeling. After working all day, dealing with traffic and stopping to run errands, opening your front door and stepping into your own warm and comfy space feels so good. Kicking off your shoes, settling down in your favorite chair or couch and leaning back into the pillow as you exhale out the long day can do wonders. This can inspire feelings of accomplishment for tasks completed and feeling blessed to have a warm comfy home to return to.

Keywords: relief, blessed, achievement, peace, comfort, nurture, accomplishment, relaxed, happy, grateful

Statement 12 - Having my dog/cat/pet greet me at the door when I get home makes me feel so loved, missed, appreciated and grateful for their presence in my life. If only people were as kind to us as our animals are. They ask for nothing but your love, kindness, food and shelter and in return, they give back so much more. Being happily greeted by your be-furred, be-finned, be-feathered or reptilian friend(s) and family member(s) when you walk in the door can lift the entire day's cares away as you gratefully cuddle with them and return their love. If you are trying to bring nurturing caring people into your life, these are the emotions to evoke when launching your intentions.

Keywords – nurtured, affection, loved, comforted, security, appreciated, joyful

Statement 13 – Exercising makes me feel energized/youthful/calm. I envy those who can run 5 miles or punch a bag for an hour and come back more energized than when they left. Some can even be at the gym at 5, work out for an hour, take a shower and head off to work feeling strong and ready to take on the day. If you are one of those people, that feeling of energy that you get can help you to power up before launching your intentions. Others feel calm and relaxed after exercising having sweated out their stress lifting weights or doing aerobic activity. Feeling calm and emotionally carefree is also a great way to begin because you won't be burdened by stress or emotional anxiety.
Keywords - energized, strong, healthy, powerful, invigorated, calm, peaceful, centered, relaxed

The extra added bonus of using the above statements to help evoke the emotions your LOA system needs is that you probably do some of these things frequently already. This can help you to get your subconscious to accept these feelings as "normal". Most people check for their pay deposits regularly, put gas in the car, see their family, go to bed, etc. Because these are emotions that your subconscious will recognize, the odds of it accepting these emotions as normal can go up much more than trying to introduce new methods that it doesn't understand.

But what if I haven't done some of those things on the list but need the emotions they inspire?
If you can't relate to some of the questions on the list and/or need an extra boost to really get the positive feelings going, there are other methods that may help.

Songs
Songs can bring up emotions from us that we may not normally feel. Recently I was bopping my head to Missy Elliot's song, "WTF". Pharrell's part came on and he was bragging about what a great artist he was. Listening to him and engaging in the music and the emotions behind his words made me feel like I was great too, at least for that moment. Even after the song was over, I kept singing his part and dancing around feeling more energized than I had in a while. Songs carry the emotions of the artist singing them and you can piggy back those emotions to help you get into the emotionally energetic state you need to be in when launching your intentions.

Make a list of songs that motivate you and inspire you with that emotion you need to fuel your intentions.

What songs make you feel happy?

What songs make you feel the love you want to feel in your current or next relationship?

What songs make you want to dance/exercise?

What songs inspire you to prosperity?

What songs make you feel beautiful?

What songs make you feel powerful?

What songs bring out your creativity?

What songs make you feel peaceful?

Movies
Not into music? Movies can also inspire within us all sorts of helpful emotions. Those who are into the fast car type movies may feel the excitement and thrill that the actors project as they pretend to dangerously race down fictional streets and highways to get away from the bad guys or the police. That thrilled and excited feeling can inspire just the energy and excitement you need to put into your intentions.

Perhaps you like romantic comedies because they make you feel that true love can be yours too if you just hang in there. If you are casting intentions to find a new love, these are just the emotions that may give your LOA system the extra oomph it needs to get the job done.

Do you like watching mysteries, enjoy trying to outsmart the bad guys with the detectives, analyzing the clues and figuring out who the guilty party is before the end of the movie? That feeling you get when you successfully determine who the bad guy is and proclaim, "I knew it!" to those watching the movie with you is not just a feeling of triumph. It took real mental work to study everything and figure out who the guilty party is. This is exactly the type of mental work that can help you analyze your own situation and figure a way out of it.

Make a list of those movies that inspire the emotions that you need to help you get extra miles down the road of your journey.

Books
Perchance you like to snuggle up with a good book and immerse yourself in the story, engaging with the emotions of the heroine/hero and/or their sidekicks. Do you like books about epic battles and feel like you're on the battlefield with the characters, fighting your way to victory? Do you like books filled with romance or books that take you into a magical realm complete with dragons, fairies, and other enchanting beings? Books are another tool that can inspire the emotions you need to help successfully navigate your journey.

So does that mean I have to re-watch a whole movie or re-read a whole book before launching an intention?
No, all you have to do is remember how watching the movie or reading the book made you feel and use that memory to jumpstart or enhance the desired emotion.

Actual Memories
Most of us have a memory of feeling the way we may need to feel now. If you don't connect to any of the scenarios above, search your memory banks to come up with a time that you felt confident, beautiful, smart, prosperous, etc. It doesn't matter how young you were, what matters is that you can still get in touch with and connect to the positive feeling the memories evoke.

Emotional Shapeshifting Exercise 2

After choosing the applicable emotion and the memory that will help you to achieve that state, bring up that memory and fully engage in the emotion. Immerse yourself in it as if it were yesterday and let those wonderful feelings flow through you.

Practice with several memories to see which one does the best job and make a note of it. Take a few minutes each day to engage in the memory so that the feelings become stronger. Once you are comfortable with being able to pull up a memory and engage in the emotions, take your practice a step further and try to sustain the emotion without recalling the memory. Just do this a few minutes even a few seconds at a time until you can do it and hold the feeling for at least 5 minutes but preferably for 20 minutes. But even if you can just do the 5, it can still help you to achieve your goals.

CHAPTER 10

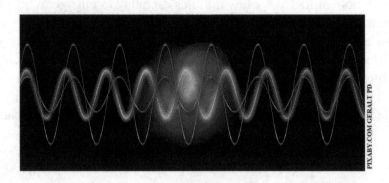

How to Maintain a Positive Attitude & Raise Your Energetic Frequency

In this section, we will discuss the importance of maintaining a positive attitude and effective ways to do that. Before we begin, please do not take the purpose of this article to mean that you will always be able to be positive and happy. Were that the case, we would not have been given emotions to let us know when we need to keep or remove things from our lives. It is after the emotion has done its job and we have addressed the challenge that it pointed out that we should return to a positive state of mind to balance out our energies and keep us strong and effective in our roles during this particular incarnation. Let us begin.

Change Your Words to Improve Your Energetic Frequency

Keeping in mind that our subconscious is greatly responsible for the type of energetic frequency we put out and therefore receive, it is also responsible for translating the things we say into what IT thinks we mean and then send out energy accordingly. Let's go over some phrases that may be inadvertently having a negative effect on your energy input and output.

I lost my job.
The economy has taken a beating, and many people have found themselves without a job and seem unable to find a new one. But saying or thinking that you "lost" your job has a subconscious vibration that it was in some way your fault. Typically when we say we lost something

154

be it a piece of jewelry, our keys or anything that we consider to be of value to us, we are taking responsibility for not paying attention to what we did with the item in question and now have to suffer the loss of it. The accompanying emotion that typically goes along with that is guilt. There is no need to point out the negative energy input and output that comes with the feeling of guilt. And even though you are innocent in causing this situation, you may still be suffering from the energetic frequency of guilt just by using the phrase "I lost my job".

Since the fault lies with the economy or the owners of the business and not with you, there is no reason for you to suffer from guilt that does not belong to you. Take a moment to acknowledge that this was not your fault and you are not broken. Now change your wording to something like, "the economy has caused me to have to switch to a new job. I attune to the positive frequencies of all the potential jobs that await me and know I will find the right one soon." Just by changing those few words, you have effectively changed your energetic input by bringing in positive emotions and outputting those same energies to help you attract a new job. It also lets both your subconscious and the Universe know that you are in a positive state and ready for a positive new job experience. Using the word "switch" means that what is gone will be replaced and that alone will help to raise your energetic frequency to a more healthy, balanced level. You are also consciously attuning to the frequencies of jobs that are right for you and this may help you to zero in on these jobs during your search for new employment.

I can't find a job/love/peace, etc.
This is another phrase that seems so simple and true but can have a vastly adverse effect on your energetic frequency. Saying or thinking that you can't find something also holds the frequency of guilt and even worse, a big dash of failure. Your subconscious may translate that as "I try and try but keep failing." Just reading those words may be making you feel bad. The way they make you feel is the way your subconscious interprets the phrase, "I can't find a job." Again, you are not the broken one. Our economy is so avoid tying into those adverse frequencies.

The same applies to finding a new love. It can be painful to feel like you will be alone forever but a little emotional shapeshifting may be able to fix that for you. Change your words to something like, "My new perfect love is seeking me as I am seeking him/her. I attune to their positive frequency and follow their flow of loving energy to our new and successful, loving and balanced relationship".

Say those words out loud and let the power of them restore your frequency to the higher level that attracts positive things and situations in your life. Feel the positive change in your energetic frequency?

If things don't change soon, I am going to ...
There are plenty of negative phrases to end that sentence such as:
• go crazy
• go broke
• be homeless
• give up
• etc.

Unfortunately, the negative phrase endings aren't the end of it. With them can come imagining all sorts of terrible things coming to pass in the future, further compromising your balanced flow of energy.

To add yet another layer of unhealthy energy, when we see our future as bleak, we may start to spend too much time thinking of the past when things seemed better and wish we could return there. Worrying about the future and wanting to hold onto the past does not leave us with much time to resolve the situations of the present. But how to keep focused on the present when it seems so painful? Start by focusing on the safety and the blessings of the moment. If panic or sadness starts to creep up on you as you worry about the future and/or grieve the past, stop and think or say things like, "For this moment, I am safe. For this moment I have food. For this moment I have shelter." List all the blessings that you have right at that very moment and feeling better, turn your mind back to the task of resolving your challenges.

Avoid negative mantras such as I don't have any money, I can't pay my bills, nobody loves me, I'm never going to find the right person

Your mind will be clearer and your resolve firmer once you free yourself up from a negatively imagined future and an irretrievable past.

Change Can Be Awesome! As far as change goes, the good news is that things are always changing and not always for the worse. Instead of saying, If things don't change…", instill positive anticipation in your words by changing them to, "I am so glad that things are changing and I request and accept those positive changes I already know are going to transform my life for the better." Smile, knowing those words are true and feel your frequency rise.

For the next few days, pay close attention to the phrases that you use to describe the situation(s) that you are trying to change. If there are negative connotations to them (and you will know because they make you feel bad) change the wording to remove those connotations and replace them with positive and hopeful words. Your energy and frequency will feel and benefit from the difference.

CHAPTER 11

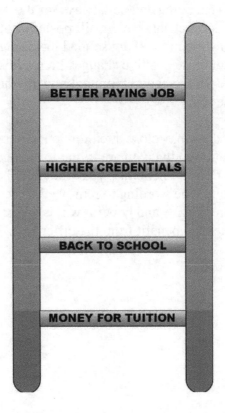

How to Clearly Convey Your Intentions - Determining What You Really Want Using the Ladder of Success

When doing Law of Attraction type work, it is important to clearly state your intentions while feeling worthy of receiving them. What is even more important is that the wording of them must reflect a crystal clear definition of what it is that you want.

It is not uncommon to hear people state that they want more abundance in their lives. When hearing that, the Universe may ask abundance of what? Love? Money? Peace? Chocolate? Perhaps you want a new job. What kind of job? At what salary and is that salary reasonable for the type of work you are looking for? If you just leave it at getting a "new job", you may be offered a career opportunity that is not in line with what you wanted.

You also want to be careful about intending for prosperity without breaking down what prosperity actually means to you. To some it means financial wealth, to others, it means having a pantry and fridge full of food, gas in the car and a nice home. To others, it could mean having lots of friends and family around. It's important to really think about it so that you are clear in what you want. If it's financial prosperity, then be sure to state that instead of just prosperity.

The ladder image above illustrates how to break down what you want, using the example of getting ahead in business but *this ladder can be used for anything you are trying to achieve.* The above ladder is set up to give an example of what a person seeking a new career or promotion might put on the ladder. Once you have broken down your career expectations, the next step is being honest about your qualifications to have such a position. Do you need extra training to qualify for the job? If yes, then part of your intentions should be to get whatever training you need to acquire the position. If training is added to the intention plate, how much will it cost and do you have the funds for it?

After investigating how much such training will cost, if you determine that you do not have the funds for it then you need to also add the amount to the ladder rung.

So a person who seeks professional advancement may start off as saying they want a better job/career but realize that there are important steps to be taken first to reach that goal. Looking at the example ladder, you can see the actual steps required.

1. Get money for tuition
2. Go back to school
3. Get a higher degree/certification
4. Apply for better job with new and improved credentials

If you use this type of ladder (and just listing the steps is also fine), you will have gone from a vague description of what you want to a finely defined list that is easy for the Universe to understand and help you achieve. The same rules apply to whatever it is you are trying to bring into your life.

Create a ladder like the one above to help you to understand what it is you actually need to state as your intention. Then focus your LOA system on what is listed on the first rung until it is achieved then move onto the next rung. This will give you a clear map to your desired goals and help you achieve it step by step.

Removing the causes of adversity
What about getting rid of the things you don't want in your life? Instead of focusing on what you want to achieve, you may be focused on getting rid of those people or things that seem to be holding you back. Removing the causes of adversity is a good thing but can be just slightly trickier because you don't want to word your intentions in a negative way such as "I don't want to be in bad relationships anymore" or "I don't want to smoke anymore." Remember that when stating your intentions, you must put your emotions behind it. Stating things that you don't want may trigger the very adverse emotions invoked by that situation. Then you could end up putting alarm emotions into the process which can seriously impact your results. If you state you don't want to be in bad relationships anymore, the pain you felt in those relationships may come through and that is the energy you are putting out into the Universe.

Instead of saying what you don't want, do the opposite and state what you do want. You want a great relationship with someone you can trust that will love you as much as you love them (add the finer details such as how they look, what they like to do, etc.). Instead of saying you want to quit smoking, change it to you want to be healthier and breathe better and feel the relief of feeling that way. This way your intention is clear and you inject a positive emotion behind it.

Hopefully, you are now well on your way to making your new intention manifestation list. Remember, keep your intentions clear, put positive emotions behind it and your dreams will manifest much more quickly.

Retraining the Mind Exercise

If you practiced exercises on in the previous chapters, you should be ready for the next step. Create a ladder that reflects the steps you need to take to get what you want. Look at the first rung of the ladder and bring up a memory or use the other techniques given to evoke the desired emotion. When fully engaged in the emotion look at the first rung on your ladder while continuing to engage in the emotions, letting your subconscious know what you want in both mental and emotional language.

Next, think of something that you are truly grateful for to flood yourself with that emotion and then state out loud or mentally, "this is what I want to achieve" and smile as gratitude courses through you. Now take action by doing what you need to do to achieve the first rung.

CHAPTER 12

Working With the Universe to Achieve Your Goals

Now that we have a clearly defined list of intentions we will take another step to increase the effectiveness of your intention manifestation practice. The next step towards helping you achieve your goals is the commitment to help the Universe to help you. The Universe is more than willing to assist you in making your dreams a reality, but you must also do your share of the work. Take your list of intentions and if possible, draw a line down the middle of the page. Use a separate piece of paper if necessary. Look at each item and then in the new column you have drawn or the separate page, write out what you intend to do to help ensure your success. Let's say your intention is to quit smoking. Write out a plan to achieve this such as speaking to your doctor about options, researching nicotine patches, books or natural ways to quit. Draw up a reasonable plan that you know you can effectively work. Some quit smoking methods allow you to quit gradually so if you know you may have a hard time going cold turkey, one of these types of plans may be right for you.

If your goal is to lose weight, write out a plan that you will be able to stick with. Research different eating plans and choose the ones that will allow you to eat the type of foods that you like. Take a look at your schedule and come up with a reasonable exercise plan that will work with your free time. If your schedule is full, you may have to get up earlier or dedicate some of your lunch hour towards taking a walk. Now is the time to figure it out so that when you are ready to launch your intentions, your plan will already be written out and ready for you.

For those of you looking for love, you need a plan too. If you've been looking for a while, then your current plan is not working. Go over it and figure out what you can do differently. Write down your hobbies and interests and then look for social clubs or meet up groups that cater to them. A great place to start is http://www.meetup.com They offer groups that cater to many types of interests and like-minded individuals. You might even find the mate you've been looking for. Can't find a group you like? Start your own. Meetup lets people in your area know about your group and soon you can have like-minded people coming to you by joining your group. For those of you just re-entering the market, the same rule applies. Use your own interests as a guide to finding a mate. Write down everything you are looking for in a person and then use it as a mirror. Ask yourself, can these same wonderful attributes be found in you? If not, work on those things that you can improve about yourself. After all, it is only fair to be able to give what you hope to receive. I've included a more detailed, "Design Your Perfect Partner" section in chapter 14.

At the bottom of your page, write: I will help the Universe to help me reach my goals. Sign your name to it and get to work. In chapter 13 are instruction on how to design your perfect mate which may also help you bring in the person of your dreams.

CHAPTER 13

Lift off! Launching your intentions

Happy New Beginnings! You have worked so hard to retrain your subconscious, increase your sense of worthiness, clearly convey your intentions and agreeing to work with the Universe/Spirit to help you achieve your goals. Now that you are ready, it is time to launch your intentions and taste the sweetness of success. Once you learn the launch steps routine, it takes about 15 minutes in total. To begin, however, try to give yourself 20-30 minutes until you have a good handle on it. If your subconscious tries to tell you that you don't have that extra time, ask yourself the big questions: **What's it worth to me to have _____ in my life?** Strengthen your resolve and have at it.

On my website is a "What's it worth to me?" banner that you can download which will be discussed at the end of this chapter. It will help to prepare you for your subconscious trying to change your mind. Of course, life happens and you truly may not have the time to devote to this every day but do it as often as you can. Baby steps are okay, so try for at least 3 days a week.

Have the following ready:
 ✓ A list of at least ten things you are thankful for

✓ Your clear intentions
✓ Clear memories that convey the desired emotion into your intentions.
✓ Any props such as your vision board, sound effects, etc.

Choose your space – Commandeer a space where you won't be disturbed, preferably for at least 20 minutes but utilize whatever time you can get for yourself. It can be out in your backyard, on your deck or balcony, out in nature, in your car or in your bedroom and even your bathroom. It is your sacred space, so you get to choose where you want it to be.

Clear your space - Prepare your sacred space, clearing it of adverse energies with sage, boiled or smoke. You can dab clove oil on the walls to remove adverse energies or boil whole cloves as well to sweep your space clear of interfering energy. You can also clear it in your own spiritual modality or however you feel comfortable.
Save time tip - create space clearing candles by dabbing clove or sage oil on a candle in the color that represents purity to you. Add your intentions that it is to clear your space of all adverse energy. This way you can just light it while doing your daily launch and put it out when not in use. Just make sure to restate your intention for pure space each time you light it.

Clear yourself –
If possible, take a cleansing bath or shower and ask the Element of Water to cleanse you on all levels, emotionally, physically, spiritually, mentally, ethically and throughout your chakra systems.
Save time tip - If you don't have time to take a bath or shower, create a cleansing mist by mixing lavender oil in a small spray bottle. How much oil you use depends on the bottle size and your preference. I use about 20 drops of oil in a 16 ounce bottle of distilled water. Try to use distilled water since it will help to extend the shelf life. You can also use whatever scent that you feel represents protection, clearing, and balance. Do your initial programming by placing your hands around the bottle and state your intention. You can say something like this:

"Dear Element of Water, Dear Oil of Lavender, please marry your energies and remove and dissolve all adverse energies in and around me and on all levels of my being. Please send them into the Light to be healed, resolved and recycled and restore me to Divine Peace and Balance. Thank you." Then keep it handy to spritz yourself before your intention work. The best way is to spray over your head so that the mists comes down and covers both the front and back of your body. Hold the bottle over your head and say, "Please cleanse, heal, balance and protect me" as you spritz yourself. This enhances the programming of the mist as it covers you. Repeat this 2 more times and notice how much better you feel. You can also carry it with you or keep in your desk at work to clear you and/or your space when you feel bogged down in adverse energy.

Continue your prep:
- ✓ Send any alarm emotions into the Light
- ✓ Quiet down the mind chatter
- ✓ Remove the adverse cords that may be attached to you and strengthen up your chakras.
- ✓ **Save time tip**: If you don't have time to do the cord removal at least lightbulb your chakras to strengthen them and your energy up
- ✓ Balance the body, mind, and spirit
  (You can find these exercises in chapter 4)

Take out your list of things that you are grateful for. State each one out loud or mentally and thank the Universe/Spirit for each of them. Not only does this convey gratitude to the Universe/Spirit but it also reinforces for you exactly how blessed you are and therefore how worthy you have already been deemed by the spiritual powers that be. This helps to enforce your own inner sense of worthiness which is a key component in successful intention work.

Take out your list of intentions. If you like you can ask the Universe/Spirit or your Deity to help you to bring your intentions to fruition.

Emotionally Shapeshift and Launch Your Intentions
1. Recall the memory that evokes the desired emotion
2. Immerse yourself in the memory and strengthen the feelings of desired emotion

3. Look at your ladder of success and the rung you are working on.
4. State or think your intention
5. Recheck your emotions to make sure you are still engaged with the proper emotion needed. If not bring up the memory again to refill you with the emotion
6. Engage additional props as needed, gazing at your vision board and or utilizing sound effects while feeling that emotion
7. State or think your intention again while engaging as many senses as possible
8. Daydream, imagine, visualize, pretend that your goal is attained and live in that moment. Literally, shapeshift your consciousness for a few moments, feeling the accomplishment of the future while riding the wave of your beneficial emotions from your past.
9. Take a deep breath and exhale, releasing your intention to the Universe for fulfillment and finish by saying "so it is."
10. If you engaged Spirit for help, thank them for their kind service to you. If you like, you can make an offering of a flower, coin or the gift of your choice to show gratitude.
11. Do a quick lightbulbing over the chakras to get them re-fueled and rebalanced.
12. If possible, immediately go back to your ladder and get started working on what you need to do to achieve the intention on the rung you are working on. Remember, taking actions is extremely important to manifest your goals more quickly. If you can't get to do the work right at that moment, then it is okay to come back later and work on it. The most important thing is to do the clearing and meditative intention work which takes approximately 15 minutes using the time-saving tips once you get the hang of the routine. For best results, do this within 30 minutes of waking up and within 30 minutes of going to bed which is when the subconscious is more receptive. Don't pressure yourself if you can't do it twice a day, every day. Just once a day will be effective and surely you can find 15 minutes in a day to work on your launch.

13. Record any progress you make in your journal so that you can focus on your achievements. Seeing results no matter how small will boost your confidence, thereby strengthening your power. It also helps to train the subconscious to start to accept new programming. As you progress, you may find that new ideas come to you or people who can help you suddenly pop up in your life. Record these as well, particularly the new ideas that you can follow up on and incorporate into your law of attraction practice.
14. When time permits, you can incorporate candles, oils, herbs and incense into your practice as well to enhance and strengthen the energy of your intentions. I also suggest searching the internet as well for books, videos and articles on these topics since it's important to find information sources that resonate with your custom beliefs.

Think about it or let it go?
There are those that believe that once an intention has been cast for fulfillment, you should not think of it anymore because that could impede the process. For those that can release their intention and put it out of their minds, that's awesome. For those of you who can't help but think about it and wonder how it's going, that's fine too. As I keep saying, everything has to be custom to you. Now, if you are wondering about the status of your intention manifestation in a worried state, that's an entirely different story. It is natural to be anxious for a positive outcome when in a hard situation but you also don't want to send adverse emotional energy chasing after all of the positive energy that you have put out. If this happens, release the worry using the exercises in chapter 5 and emotionally shapeshift into hope. Hope is probably one of the most powerful emotions there is. It signifies belief that things can change for the better and that belief is what can turn everything around. Hope is a beautiful thing and an awesome energy to immerse yourself in. Also, when your mind keeps coming back to your intentions, add the sentence, "With each thought, I achieve my goals for which I am truly grateful." Then go about what you need to do to make it happen.

* ENHANCED LOVE LIFE * GOOD HEALTH * PEACE * SUCCESS * PROSPERITY *

WHAT'S IT WORTH TO ME?

*A NEW HOME * A NEW CAREER * PHYSICAL, ENERGETIC & MENTAL FITNESS *

How to Prepare for Your Subconscious Trying to Change Your Mind

Before I start this section, I want to quickly let you know that the full color version of the banner that you see above you is available for you to print out free of charge. You can affix it to your walls, your refrigerator, wherever you will see it when your subconscious tries to talk you out of striving for your new and desired life. You can also take a picture of it to keep on your phone so that you have it handy during moments of weakness when you are outside of your home. You can get it on my website at http://www.healinghennagoddess.com and then click on "Free Gifts" and download the WHAT'S IT WORTH TO YOU 2 PORTRAIT FOR PRINTING.PDF

We've already gone over how your subconscious tries to keep everything "normal" so it's a pretty fair bet that it will try to get you to go back to what it feels is your normal state of being. It may try in many different ways such as throwing all the things you have to do in your head in an effort to get you to feel that you just don't have the 15 minutes to do your intention work. If you are trying to lose weight, it may try to convince you that you don't have time to exercise or make sure that you notice every time you come in a range of tasty and fattening foods. If you want to go back to school, it may try to make you feel overwhelmed by pointing out all of the courses you have to take, the time you have to put in, the sacrifices you will have to make and so on. It is said that it typically takes doing something 21 times before it becomes a habit so for the first month of your launch, you have to be extra disciplined and answer it in a way that it understands and that will make you feel better at the same time. Here are some examples:

Weight Loss
You're in the grocery store buying healthier foods to lose weight and your subconscious starts pointing out all the cakes and pies that are available or whatever fattening food is your biggest downfall. To fight

169

back, think something like, "Technically I can have whatever I want in moderation. Let me just get used to my new plan and then I will add in a day where I will allow myself "treat" food." Be sure to say, treat and not cheat because the energy of the words cheat and cheating can suggest that you are doing something wrong and can lower your vibration with alarm emotions such as guilt, disappointment, shame, etc. The word treat has a far better vibration. It suggests something that you earned, something that is good and helps to keep your vibration at a nice high frequency. By assuring yourself that you are not in a health food cage but can figure out a way to add in treats without stopping your program, can help to ease the way. Also, when that craving for fattening food hits, immediately start thinking about the new (or old) clothes that you will be able to fit into and how much better you will look and feel by eating healthier. Shapeshift by remembering a time you looked and felt great and immerse yourself in that memory then think about how great it will feel to be in a healthier body. When you are thinking about your new and healthier body, the uplifted emotions that go along with it flood your system. This further lets your subconscious know what you want your new "normal" state to be.

If you have added in a fitness program, expect your subconscious to point out how sore you will be and/or insist that you won't have time to stay on track with them. It might even cause you to procrastinate doing other tasks so that you really won't have time. Before you start your exercise program, figure out how much time you can realistically put into exercise and on what days and times of the week that you will be able to do so. If you have an erratic schedule, then try for first thing in the morning even if it means you have to get up 20 minutes earlier. As the banner above say, what's it worth to you? Is it worth it to be healthier and in better shape? Exercise can help combat many illnesses such as diabetes, heart disease and may even help to prevent it if you are at risk. Imagine how much easier it will be to do physical tasks. It's important to remind the subconscious why you are doing this in the first place so that you can be healthier, stronger and even calmer since exercise can burn away stress as well as calories. Even just 20 minutes three times a week can benefit you and you can exercise while you watch your favorite TV shows and kill two birds with one stone.

Going to school
Expect your subconscious to complain about how much time it's going
to take, especially if you work and can only go part time. Let's say you
are going for an associate's degree and because you work, it will take
you approximately three years to complete it. To counter your
subconscious' harping on the amount of time it will take, remind
yourself that time is going to pass anyway. So in three years, you can be
kicking yourself because you would have finished your degree if you
had stuck with it *or* in three years you can be graduating triumphantly,
proud of your perseverance and dedication to improving your life and
ready to go for that higher salaried career.

Starting a business
Your subconscious will probably have a field day with this one. Expect
it to bring up how long it might take to start making money and the
uncertainty of success. How maybe you hate your current job but at least
its stable. Expect it to bring up all the sacrifices you will have to make,
the long hours you will have to put in, the expenses that go along with it
while waiting to make a profit and so on. If you are currently working
for someone else, you can stave off a lot of problems by doing as much
as you can before leaving your present job. You can file your business
papers, seek out the best space for your new shop or outfit your home
office if you are going to be working from home.

You can arrange your contacts, look into marketing techniques and
devise strategies to make your business take off. If you are in a heart-
based business, research heart-based marketing so you don't have to
worry about being cutthroat and competitive but can build your business
in a way that is in harmony with your soul. You can study the websites
of successful businesses to get ideas and buy books on the same subject.

You can look into suppliers, bookkeeping software, all while you are
already earning a living. If you are currently unemployed and have
decided to start your own business, then your subconscious may try to
convince you to keep looking for a regular job and that by starting your
own business, you could be heading towards financial disaster. The way
to counter that is to remind yourself that if necessary, you can find a job,
even if it's one that you don't particularly like but one that will help pay
the bills. Then start thinking about how happy you will be once your

business takes off. Even the planning and implementing phase can be exciting because you are taking your future into your own hands and the sky is the limit! Think of how hard you worked for previous employers and helped them to succeed. Think of how now you will put that effort into your own dreams and how that will not just feed your wallet but feed your soul as well. As you think of these things, your emotional state is elevated, and it's a reminder to your subconscious in its own language of the new normal that you are seeking. In the resources section, I recommend a great book that helped me to launch my business from a literal shoestring which I spoke about in the beginning of this book. You can do this!

These are just a few examples. No matter what it is that you are trying to do, your perseverance will pay off. Just be ready to have to work to get your subconscious on the same page, and if you momentarily get distracted, that's okay just reaffirm what achieving this is worth to you and get right back at it.

CHAPTER 14

OTHER TIPS AND TRICKS AND WHAT TO DO WHILE YOU WAIT

While you wait for your desires to manifest, here are some things to do to help keep you patient and help to move you further along your path.

Walk in Divine Timing – It really is true that patience is a virtue. Some people are naturally patient, but there are many of us who are not, especially when waiting for that much-needed breakthrough to arrive. When impatience rears its head, then it can help to focus on the fact that your blessings will come to you in Divine timing. That means if you are waiting for the $500 you need to pay a bill by the 25th and it's the 20th of the month, instead of allowing anxiety to take over repeat the following phrase:
There is no such thing as time. There is only Divine timing. I walk in Divine timing.

By saying this, I have found that it takes the pressure off and helps to relax the body mind and spirit. It also works well when you are running late and stressed out sitting in traffic.

I have a video tutorial that you can watch and follow along on my YouTube Channel. Just go to **www.youtube.com** and put in my name to bring up my page.

Page: Rhonda Harris Choudhry
Playlist: Mini Magick & Energy Work Classes
Video: How to Bend Time & Walk in Divine Timing

Work with the Days and Planets to Help Fuel Your Success

Speaking of timing, each day of the week represents a planet and each planet represents properties that can help you with what you are trying to achieve. You may have created a list of tasks to complete that might seem overwhelming. You can break up the list into pieces and complete the tasks on the days that carry the energy to support your efforts.

Monday (Moon): Healing, psychic abilities, emotional balance, sleep, spirituality and working with the element of water.

Tuesday (Mars): Defense, courage, strength, protection, assertiveness, confidence and working with the element of fire.

Wednesday (Mercury): Accruing wisdom, travel, mental agility and strength, communication, *business and commerce, and working with the element of air.
*Back in the olden days, they didn't have planes, trains, and automobiles. Merchants relied on sailing to the places they vended their wares and needed the element of air that Mercury represents to fill their sails and get them to where they needed to go.

Thursday (Jupiter): Good luck, expansion, prosperity, socializing and having fun, networking and working with the element of air.

Friday (Venus) and (Neptune):
Venus: Love, wealth, compassion, creativity, fertility, beauty, sexuality and working with the element of earth.
Neptune: Healing, creativity particularly writing since Neptune is great for spinning stories, meditation particularly on vision boards since Neptune can help you believe that these things will be yours. Neptune is the planet of illusion so for those who have a hard time with mustering the required beliefs and visualizations of the future they seek to have, this planet can help you immerse yourself in your dreams of success

which can cause the necessary emotional shapeshifting to get you what you want. Neptune represents the element of water.

Saturday (Saturn): Wealth, protection, business success, restricting adverse influences, grounding and centering and working with the element of earth.

Sunday (Sun): Success, good health, vitality, wealth, enlightenment, energy, resolving legal matters and working with the element of fire.

Of course, if your intuition tells you to do something on a specific day, then by all means, follow your intuition. It is here to guide you and protect you.

Be What You Eat

Love Attraction   Wealth Attraction   Success   Mental Power

Fruits and vegetables contain many nutrients and health benefits that our bodies need. They also symbolize many of the energies that you are seeking to bring into your own energetic field to improve your life. For example, an apple represents Venus, so if you are looking for love or want to enhance your beauty, you can charm the apple with your intention and then go ahead and eat it. Oranges represent the Sun which also represents success. Grapes can enhance your mental power while oatmeal can attract wealth. When you eat, the energy of the food becomes a part of your own energetic field so go ahead and program your food so that it nourishes and enhances your energy as well as your physical body. I won't go into the spiritual properties of all of the different foods since there are books already published that are great sources of information. In the resource section in the back of this book,

I've included my favorite book on foods and herbs that will help you to know the energies they carry for you to utilize. You can also quickly find what energies foods carry simply by typing, "spiritual properties of _____ (oats, cherries, cucumbers, etc.). You might be surprised at all of the beneficial energies that are in foods you eat every day.

First Cleanse the Food -
Of course, before you begin charming your food, it's important to clear it of toxic energy first. There is much in the news about "eating clean" but if your food is laden with the alarm energies of those who handled it before you, then eating clean is not an option. When you go through the produce aisle, look at all the other customers handling and squeezing the fruits and vegetables. Those who are in a bad or sad mood can transfer that energy into the piece of fruit that you are about to purchase and eat. This means that you get to ingest their toxic energy giving you more than you bargained for and not in a good way. Also consider how many other people have touched your food including the farm workers, packers, distributors, truck drivers, store personnel, etc. There is no way to know what kind of moods these people were in when they handled your food, so it is best to cleanse it just in case. Of course, it's not just fruits and vegetables that need to be cleared. All food that you ingest has been subject to the energies of all who have come in contact with it. Instructions to spiritually cleanse your food are given below.

Cleansing your water and all fluids you bring into your body is equally important. An awesome Doctor of Alternative Medicine named Masaru Emoto has effectively demonstrated how emotions affect water structure. Here is a link to an article that shows the difference in water crystals that have been subjected to loving emotions and those subjected to hateful emotions. The difference is astounding! He also points out that we are made of 70% water. After looking at his pictures, consider how much your alarm emotions are affecting the fluids that runs through your entire body.

Here is the link to that article:
http://www.unitedearth.com.au/watercrystals.html
For those of you reading this in print, type "The Water Crystals of Masaru Emoto" into your browser and the article should come up or type in the link above.

176

Now take another moment to consider everyone who has come in contact with your bottled water, soda, coffee, etc. and the alarm emotions that they may have been projecting as they touched your drink. All I can say is YUCK! Thankfully, the article also demonstrates the healing and beneficial effects of putting positive thoughts and affirmations into water before you drink it. You can use your own prayers or techniques to clear your food and drinks, and you can also check out my video on how to spiritually cleanse food and drinks to eat clean.

I have a video tutorial that you can watch and follow along on my YouTube Channel. Just go to **www.youtube.com** and put in my name to bring up my page.

YouTube page: Rhonda Harris Choudhry
Playlist: Empath Training Mini Class Series
Video: How to Spiritually Cleanse your Food to Eat Clean

Here are the written instructions for those who do not have access to the internet or prefer written instructions:

<u>Cleansing Food</u>

Cleansing and charging your food and drinks with spiritual energy not only makes it healthier for you to ingest but will also empower you with purified nutrients. Try this by taking a cracker, piece of bread or any food and split it in half. Put one half to the side and do the following with the other and then taste them both. You may be astounded at the difference.

1. Hold the half cracker/bread or plate of food in your hands.
2. Imagine a clear blue sky with a big fiery Sun shining down.
3. Imagine the Sunlight flowing into your food, into your plate, and through the plate into your hands.
4. Imagine a starry night sky with a big beautiful Full Moon.
5. Imagine the light of the Moon streaming into your food, into the plate, and through the plate into your hands

6. Imagine the many lights from stars streaming into the food, into the plate, and through the plate into your hands.
7. Now the starlight retracts with our thanks
8. Now the Moonlight retracts with our thanks
9. Now the Sunlight retracts with our thanks
10. Say or think, "this food is restored to Divine optimum nutrition for my optimum good health

Your food is purified and ready to eat. Take a taste of the food you just cleansed. Then take a taste of the food you put to the side so that you can taste the difference.

If you are a reiki practitioner, you can also use the cho ku rei symbols to cleanse your food and beverages.

<u>Cleansing your drinks</u>
First taste your drink so that you will have a basis of comparison.
1. Make a small "d" with your right hand by placing the middle finger, ring finger and pinky against the thumb and while pointing the index finger up.
2. Place your hand to the right of your beverage and turn it so that the index finger horizontally pointing at the space directly in front of you.
3. Place your left hand with fingers together on the left side of your beverage and also turn it so that the fingers are all pointing straight out horizontally.
4. Position your hands so that they are at the center of the beverage.
5. Raise your hands to the top of the beverage
6. Lower your hands to the bottom of the beverage
7. Bring your hands back up to center
8. Hold for about 5 seconds.

Taste your beverage and feel the difference in the weight, texture, and taste.

You can also use this method to clear your bathwater as well except that you will position your hands over the center of the filled tub and move back and forth accordingly.

Now that your food and drinks are cleaned up go ahead and program them to help you with your goals. Place your hands around the food and say, "I invoke and evoke, request and accept all of your wonderful, positive, powerful, properties, gifts, blessings and protections of this food, including but not limited to

_____, (state the energies of the food that you are activating), Thank you"

Color Your Drinks, Yourself and Your Space

Colors have amazing energy. Just think about how powerful your color based chakras and auras are. You can add the energy of color to your life to really amp up your energy with the energies they can convey to you. On my website under "Free Gifts" you will find a color chart that you can print out, laminate and use it to:

- ✓ Put under your drinks to saturate them with the color to get the energy you want.
- ✓ Surround and infuse yourself with the color that represents whatever energy you are trying to obtain.
- ✓ Infuse your room with the energy of the color that will help to support you as you work on your goals.

Before you use them, though, it is important to create your own custom definitions of color. To some people, the color blue may mean peace while to others it may mean prosperity. The color white may mean healing to some but protection to others. In order to get the most out of using the colors, the color definitions must be one that you believe in, not the definitions of other people.

For those of you who are mental based, just writing down what the colors mean may be enough. However many people who are "feeling" or empaths maybe find making mental decisions challenging. This is because their decision making processes are based on their feelings and not their thoughts. If you are one of these people, it may be best for you to test out how the color actually makes you feel so that you can correctly identify the ones that carry the energy that you need. So for example, if you think the color pink means nurturing energy, take a moment to gaze at it and be aware of the response your body gives you. Does it actually feel like nurturing energy or something else? Write down the way it makes you feel so that you have a custom color chart that resonates harmoniously with your energetic field.

You can also use crayons or markers to create your own chart. If you choose to download it, make three copies. One for your drinks, another to infuse color into your energetic field and one or more to hang in your room(s) to infuse them with color.

I also suggest obtaining a dry erase marker with built-in eraser. These are the markers used on white boards and can be found at any office supply store or ordered online. I use them on my laminated color charts because one color can mean different things to me. So for example, I have Lyme disease which comes with chronic fatigue. Since red represents energy to me, I have had great success writing the word "energy" on the red circle, putting my glass over it and drinking it down. My energy levels go up and I can get much more done. However, red also means protection and defense to me so if I feel I need that particular energy, with my dry erase marker I can erase the word energy and replace it with "protection" so that when I ingest it, I project energy to defend me from the inside out. I can also mix the energies by writing both protection and energy in the circle. I don't suggest mixing more than two or three energies at a time. Having the marker with the eraser will allow you to change the definition of the color to create the energy(ies) that you need at that particular moment.

Now let's say you create your color definitions and then decide you want to surround yourself with the color of peace. If you define peace as blue and go to gaze at it but find yourself staring at another color instead, that could be your soul saying that peace would be nice but what you really need is represented in the color that keeps calling you. Identify what that color means to you so that you know what it is that your soul craves and then feed it the color it wants.

1. To download the color chart .pdf, go to www.healinghennagoddess.com and click on Free Gifts and then the COLOR CHART.pdf to download it.
2. Make a list of your color definitions.
3. Choose a color from the chart that represents the energy you want based on your own color definitions.

Using the Color Chart for Drinks

A. In the center of the colored circle write the word that represents the energy you want to acquire.
B. Place your glass of water on top of the color and word for at least 60 seconds. When you first begin using the chart, experiment with the amount of time that you leave your drink on the color and make notes so that you know how much time works for you and what level of energy you get based upon the amount of time the drink was left on the color. This helps you to get even more in touch with your own custom needs.
C. Drink your drink and enjoy the energy.

Using the Color Chart to Infuse Your Energetic Field with the Energy You Need

A. Choose a color from the chart that represents the energy that you need.
B. In the center of the color, write the word that represents the type of energy that you need.
C. Gaze at the color and imagine it safely surrounding and infusing you and your energetic field with it until you are satisfied with the amount of energy you are feeling.

Using the Color Chart for Infusing Your Room/Space with Color

A. Choose a color from the chart that represents the energy that will support you with the work you are doing such as diligence, success, focus, etc. You can also just choose a relaxing color or a color which represents purity to cleanse your space.
B. Write the word that represents the energy you are looking for in the center of the circle.
C. Affix the chart to a wall or hold it in your hands and gaze at it while imagining it is filling the room with the color and energy you are going for.

As an extra added bonus, wear the colors that represent what you are trying to achieve. Even if you have to wear a certain uniform or color at work, you can wear underwear in the color that will help to support your energy and your goals.

I have a video tutorial that you can watch and follow along on my YouTube Channel. Just go to **www.youtube.com** and put in my name to bring up my page.

YouTube page: Rhonda Harris Choudhry
Playlist: Empath Training Mini Class Series
Video: How to Use Colors to Change Your Energy and Heal Your Life

Plant an intention garden

If you've got a green thumb, you can also grow plants that represent what you want and start an intention garden. Consider creating an intention garden to help you manifest whatever it is you are trying to bring into your life. Seeds and plants can be empowered with your intentions, and as they grow, they send out intention laden energy to help you achieve your goals. Best of all you can incorporate the flowers and even the fruits and vegetables that you were planning to use anyway, so you won't have to create any extra space in your already planned garden. You can also place crystals and gemstones in your garden to increase the power of your intentions.

Many common plants and flowers are already programmed with specific energies. All you have to do is customize those energies to fit your needs.
Here are some examples using common plants, flowers and even fruits and vegetables.

Tomatoes – Love, money, protection
Lettuce – Peace, protection, divination
Carrots – Fertility
Chrysanthemums – Protection
Honeysuckle – Promotes psychic awareness
Chili Peppers – Fidelity, breaks curses and hexes
Strawberries – Luck, love

Do you have fruit trees in your yard or planning to plant some? Trees also hold magical properties that can be used for your benefit.
Apple – Healing, love
Orange – Luck, prosperity, psychic abilities
Lemon – Love, long life, friendship
Peach – Fertility, long life, protection

Do you live in an apartment? No problem! You can grow a small herb garden that will work just as well.

Mint – Healing, protection, money
Basil – Prosperity, protection, love
Thyme – Sleep, healing, courage, health
Rosemary – Purification, healing, mental awareness

Having an intention garden doesn't take a lot of work and the potential benefits it brings are well worth the effort of growing and maintaining one.

Another alternative for those who live in an apartment is to grow wheatgrass and infuse it with your intentions. It grows easily and will last for about a month so you can start a new plant with fresh intentions preferably on or around the New Moon. Wheat represents wealth and fertility. You can use that fertility energy to plant, nurture and grow your intentions to fruition. You can then dry out the blades of grass and create an incense to burn to further your intention manifestation. Just mix it with oils and/or herbs and spices that also represent what you are trying to bring into your life.

Empower your seeds by focusing your thoughts of what you want into them. Place a piece of paper with your intention on it in the middle of the pot and then the seeds on top. Include on your written note what you want to manifest such as a car, a new job, a new mate, etc. Write as small as you can on the note so you can fit your aspirations on it.

You can use your own spiritual methods or if you need help I have a video tutorial that you can watch and follow along on my YouTube Channel. Just go to **www.youtube.com** and put in my name to bring up my page.

YouTube page: Rhonda Harris Choudhry
Playlist: Empath Training Mini Class Series
Video: How to Grow a Magick Intention Garden to Manifest Your Goals

Design Your Perfect Partner

For those of you who have been searching for the love of your life, trying to find the partner who is perfect for you may seem to have become like trying to find the Holy Grail. Perhaps you have tried many times with many people or have been alone hoping the right one would come along. Either way, it is normal to long for the one who will proudly walk beside you, support you and cherish you like the gem that you are. Take heart because there are ways to bring you the person who seems custom made just for you. With a few simple steps, you can become a love magnet, attracting people who resonate with you safely and are in harmony with what you want. Let's get started.

Change Your Words or Why You Shouldn't Ask for a Soul Mate
One of the most commonly heard wishes for love is, "I want to find my soul mate". This is understandable because it sounds like a person who was sent here to love you and support you. The truth of the matter is that the soul mate relationship is a learning relationship and unfortunately we often learn best through conflict. These types of relationships can be the I love you, I hate you, come closer, stay back, can't live with you and can't live without you, Romeo and Juliette type of relationships. They may seem miserable, but even if you try to break up with the person, the spiritual connection is so strong that you continue to feel that person's energy even when no longer in a relationship with them. The purpose of the soul mate relationship is to learn valuable lessons about life through relationships, and few things teach better lessons than conflict because conflict requires a lot of introspection, compromise, sacrifice, all lessons that we need to help our souls evolve. If you have been in a string of conflicted relationships or even just one, chances are you already have found your soul mate(s).

Another reason to avoid asking for a soul mate is that soul mates are not just romance partners nor is there just one. They can be friends, parents, relatives, co-workers, etc. all here to help you to learn and grow. Try changing your wish to, "I want to find the person who is perfect for me and who I am perfect for, who resonates with me safely and is in harmony with my life's plan and purpose and I with theirs." Just making this adjustment to your way of thinking may drastically improve who comes into your life because now the Universe knows what you really want.

The next wish to rethink is, "I want someone who will love me unconditionally". When you think about that, it's a pretty tall order. Consider what you are saying. You are effectively saying that you should be able to do whatever you want and still expect your partner to love you even if what you do hurts them. On the same token if you offer to love unconditionally then you are giving your partner license to lie, cheat and steal from you, inflict emotional pain or commit any number of nightmarish acts and that will be okay with you. That type of love is usually reserved for parents and their children. No matter what a child does, their parents may punish them but will still love them and even that is not always the case. Treat someone badly, and eventually, they will probably fall out of love with you and into the arms of someone who treats them better. Change your wish to, "I want a partner who will love, respect and support me in the same way that I will love, respect and support them." This is a much more reasonable wish and makes it clear to the Universe precisely what you truly want.

The third wish is, "I just want someone who will make me happy." Happy is a very general word and in order for the law of attraction to work it is important to be specific about exactly what it is that makes you happy. This brings us to our next step.

Change Your Type
Many of us have a certain "type" of person that we are drawn to. They may be short, tall, slim, curvy or muscular. Perhaps they have a certain way of smiling or are the serious type. They may have a certain swagger that sends heat through your entire system and draws you to them like a bee to honey. If this is has been the case, and your relationships with these "types" have not ended well, then it may be time to change your type. Of course, if you have liked a certain type for a while it might seem hard to change it, but all it takes is some introspection.

The way to start is to sit down and define exactly what you are looking for in a partner. When you do this, you start to think past the color of their eyes and/or their body type. You start to search your soul for the type of partner that you are really looking for. To start designing your perfect partner, start by asking yourself these basic questions and then fill in the blanks yourself with what you are looking for:
  ✓ What is my perfect partner's personality like?
  ✓ What hobbies do they have?
  ✓ What are their passions?
  ✓ How do they feel about commitment?

✓ What is their idea of a perfect partnership?
✓ What is their communication style?
✓ What type of sense of humor do they have?
✓ How affectionate are they?

Start with those basics and then add your own such as what industry do they work in and now would also be a good time to add in your preferred hair and eye color, body type and unless you want to pay the freight, you might want to ask that they at least be self-supporting.

Create and Execute Your Action Plan
Now that you have better defined the type of partner you are looking for, it's time to create and execute your action plan. Take a piece of unlined paper and at the top, put My Perfect Partner. Then list all of the attributes that you came up with when designing them. Next, keep the list by your bedside and as soon as you wake up or at least within the first 30 minutes when the subconscious is more open to suggestion, read your list. As you read it, breathe life into it by imagining what it would be like to be with such a person, how it would make you feel, the joy it would bring. Then put the paper down and go about your day. If possible, at some point during the day, come back and repeat the process.

Next, do the same thing within 30 minutes of going to sleep. The reason it's best to keep it by the bedside is because it will be there when you wake up and will be there when you go to sleep. This starts the law of attraction's magnetic powers to start to attract the one you that will truly complement and make you happy.

Do Your Part
Just creating and reading your action plan is not enough. The Universe will do its part, but you still have to do yours. If you are a homebody, go out and start mingling. You can join a meetup group that has like-minded people in your area, (www.meetup.com). Just hanging out with a group of people who share your interests can open whole new doors for you. Let your trusted friends know that you are looking. You never know who has a cousin or uncle that is also looking and that you may be compatible with. Consider joining a reputable dating site. The point is to

get out there so that your perfect partner can find you. Alas, there is no magic GPS that will just guide them to your door.

Sweeten Your Life

Sometimes it can seem like if you didn't have bad luck, you would have no luck at all. Your travails may have started out with one issue such as losing your job, going through a divorce or contracting an illness and then things may have spiraled downward from there to the point that you may feel a black storm cloud must be stalking you and rains more bad luck down on you just when you thought things were about to get better. When you are inundated with so many adverse energies, it may be time to energetically sweeten your life.

Many people take salt baths when attempting to remove the adverse energies plaguing them. And that may work fine for them since they are obviously in harmony with the energy of salt. However, if you have tried this and gotten little or no improvement, then salt may not be harmonious with your own energies. Salt is a bitter substance, and if you have a lot of bitterness in your life, then you could just be adding salt to your wounds. Try countering with sugar instead. Add a tablespoon of honey with the intention that it sweeten your life and/or help you to obtain the "sweet life" that you have been looking for, to your shampoo, hair conditioner, and bath gel. Make a sugar scrub with lavender and coconut oil, lavender to bring peace to your life and coconut to purify

188

the adverse energies and protect you from any in the future. It's important to state your intentions to each ingredient to make sure it is infused with your purpose.

This can also help if you are forced to work with people who contribute to the harsh energies around you. They may be jealous of you or just like to give you a hard time. They may leave you alone but be so angry over things in their own life that their angry energy leaks into your workspace. If these are people that you are forced to work with, and you can't do anything about it, you can also wear sugar to help create the air of sweetness around you. All you need is a small plastic zipper-type lock bag that you can get in most craft stores. Take one and fill it with sugar. Hold it between your hands and say, "Be sweet to me" three times then stick it in your bra or your pocket. You will probably find that people will be nicer to you.

I have a video tutorial that you can watch and follow along on my YouTube Channel. Just go to **www.youtube.com** and put in my name to bring up my page.

YouTube page: Rhonda Harris Choudhry
Playlist: Empath Training Mini Class Series
Video: How to Make Negative People Be Sweeter to You

Get Inspired!

When I was faced with so many challenges that seemed insurmountable, I would derive inspiration by reading rags to riches stories. Reading of how some very famous and successful people overcame enormous odds of poverty, abuse, homelessness, etc., inspired me to keep going because I knew that if they could do it, so could I. You can do an internet search under rags to riches stories and find tons of them. Here is one of my favorites, https://yourstory.com/2014/05/rags-to-riches/

One of my favorite sources of inspiration is Jack Canfield, the author of *Chicken Soup for the Soul.* Despite 144 rejection letters, he kept going anyway and has now sold over 500 million copies and is a constant source of inspiration to at least that many people! I also love JK Rowling who was extremely impoverished while writing the beloved Harry Potter series. No need to point out how successful she became despite the hard times she lived through. Wanting to write books has always been a dream of mine and reading their stories gave me the courage to write and see it through. You too can find inspiration to do whatever you want. Look especially for success stories from those in the fields that you wish to engage and grow in and then persevere and make it happen. You can do it! You can achieve your dreams! I have full confidence in you ♥

****

Resources

If you want to contact the author, you may do so through her website at www.healinghennagoddess.com
Facebook: https://www.facebook.com/GoddessRhonda/
YouTube:
https://www.youtube.com/channel/UChWH7bUPjWddzI6agjaePVA
Email: goddessrhonda@healinghennagoddess.com
You can also check out upcoming classes, download the free gifts mentioned in this book, set up readings, counseling, hypnotherapy and healing sessions and find links to free video tutorials for empaths and spiritually minded people on her site.

Online Temple with Live Spiritual Ceremonies (especially great for solitaries who want to join in celebration with others)

Goddess Spirituality Online Temple and Learning Circle:
http://www.meetup.com/GoddessSpiritualityCircle/ or check out our archived shows at:
https://www.youtube.com/playlist?list=PLl928nB8STssfEgHaU59GYVKZlgw53O8c
(If you are reading this in print, go to YouTube and put my name in to bring up my channel. Click on playlists and then Goddess Spirituality Online Temple Services.)

Empaths and the Highly Sensitive Training

My YouTube tutorials to help Empaths and the Highly sensitive to lead a happier and healthier life:
https://www.youtube.com/playlist?list=PLl928nB8STss2qtwNPwajoxE_Jd__1Pdo
(If you are reading this in print, go to YouTube and put my name in to bring up my channel. Click on playlists and then Empath Training Mini Class Series.)

Develop Your Psychic Abilities

Here is my YouTube playlist to help you identify and enhance your psychic abilities-
https://www.youtube.com/playlist?list=PLl928nB8STssagI5hRJnaOCRFc08_EY87
(If you are reading this in print, go to YouTube and put my name in to bring up my channel. Click on playlists and then How to Raise Psychic Abilities Mini Class Series)

Prosperity/Wealth Attraction

Here is my YouTube playlist to attract more prosperity into your life: https://www.youtube.com/playlist?list=PLl928nB8STsul7Y9UE7EtG6mqGb3kCdzz
(If you are reading this in print, go to YouTube and put my name in to bring up my channel. Click on playlists and then Money, Prosperity Magick and Manifestation Mini Classes)

Psychic Self Defense and Protection

Here are is my YouTube playlist for Spiritual Protection & Cleansings Mini Energy Classes:
https://www.youtube.com/playlist?list=PLl928nB8STss_-TFgLqFrUQFXqiNey9H4
(If you are reading this in print, go to YouTube and put my name in to bring up my channel. Click on playlists and then Spiritual Protection & Cleansings Mini Energy Classes)

My Enchanted Line of Clothing, Accessories and Home Goods
Please visit Vida and check out my reiki infused garments, accessories and home goods at https://shopvida.com/collections/rhonda-harris-choudhry
If you are reading this in print, go to https://shopvida.com/ and put my name into the search and my page will come up.

Donation Request

Please support Find Me

The Find Me Group is a wonderful organization I belong to. We work to combat human trafficking and solve missing persons cases. We've brought closure and healing to so many families like yours. Find Me Group is unique in that it uses a variety of tools--including forensic science, K9 units, artificial intelligence, and psychics--to fulfill its mission. I've seen our successes first-handed, and I encourage you learn about us at our website, and donate to our 501c3 nonprofit at www.findmegroup.org/donate

Help us to help others and their families know they too are not broken!

Metaphysical Store

If you are ever in Albuquerque, Please visit this cool store for great gifts and all of your metaphysical needs:

Blue Eagle Metaphysical Emporium
2422 Juan Tabo Blvd NE
Albuquerque, NM 87112
(505) 298-3682

Spirituality Based Show and E-Zines

The Priestess View – A show I cohost that discusses what's popular in our magical world and has great guests to boot.
https://www.youtube.com/playlist?list=PLl928nB8STst0CgQuoZjMVI5
1a5otvZIn
(If you are reading this in print, go to YouTube and put my name in to bring up my channel. Click on playlists and then The Priestess View Show.)

Pagan Business News Network: http://pbnnewsnetwork.com/

Lightworker's World: http://www.lightworkersworld.com/

Note: All of the Amazon links given go to their sister site www.smile.amazon.com

This site donates a portion of your purchase to the charity of your choice at no additional cost to you. You can register your preferred charity with them and help to support them with your purchases which gives you extra good karma ☺ Of course if you choose to use the regular Amazon site, these items are also available there as well.

Herb and Food Symbolic Meanings

Cunningham's Encyclopedia of Magical Herbs by Scott Cunningham
https://smile.amazon.com/Cunninghams-Encyclopedia-Magical-Llewellyns-Sourcebook-ebook/dp/B002H8ORHU/ref=sr_1_fkmr0_1?s=books&ie=UTF8&qid=1474393087&sr=1-1-fkmr0&keywords=Cunninham%27s+encyclopedia+of+magical+herbalism#nav-subnav

Heart Based Marketing Really Worked for Me

Attracting the Perfect Customers by Stacey Hall and Jan S. Stringer
https://smile.amazon.com/s/ref=nb_sb_ss_i_6_10?url=search-alias%3Daps&field-keywords=attracting+perfect+customers&sprefix=attracting%2Caps%2C302&crid=31KC9KMBNXCOG

Connect to the Goddess

Shakti Mantras: Tapping into the Great Goddess Energy
by Thomas Ashley-Farrand
https://smile.amazon.com/Shakti-Mantras-Tapping-Goddess-Energy/dp/0345443047/ref=sr_1_1?s=books&ie=UTF8&qid=1474558788&sr=1-1&keywords=shakti+mantras

Christian Manifesting through the Bible

Old Style Conjure Working with the Bible by Starr Casas
http://www.oldstyleconjure.com/working-with-the-bible.php

Adrenaline Addict Articles:
http://mentalhealthdaily.com/2013/03/02/how-to-overcome-adrenaline-addiction-tips-from-a-former-addict/

http://www.tablegroup.com/blog/the-painful-reality-of-adrenaline-addiction

https://www.verywell.com/how-to-tell-if-youre-an-adrenaline-addict-3145035

http://www.theiflife.com/stress-making-you-fat-sick/

http://www.lifeextension.com/magazine/2011/9/Reducing-the-Risks-of-High-Cortisol/Page-01

https://www.google.com/?ion=1&espv=2#q=what%20causes%20adrenaline%20addiction

References:
Marriage in the 1600s
http://internetshakespeare.uvic.ca/Library/SLT/society/family/marriage.html

Life expectancy
http://u.demog.berkeley.edu/~andrew/1918/figure2.html

PHOTO CREDITS

Cover - PIXABY.COM PEXELS PUBLIC DOMAIN

Why Not Me? FREEIMAGES.COM/Anders Engelbol

The Pre-Reqs to Raising Your Vibration – FREEIMAGES.COM/Mihai Andoni

Weightloss:
1. Hamburger - FREEIMAGES.COM/JCB SPARES
2. Salad – FREEIMAGES.COM/ MOI CODY

Emotional Platform (less words) – FREEIMAGES.COM/Simeon Eichmann

How Your Subconscious May See Your Conscious Mind (without long nose) FREEIMAGES.COM/ DARKO NOVAKOVIC

Opening Doors to New Beginnings:
1. Scenery – FREEIMAGES.COM/ANDY LIPKE
2. Ruin Door – FREEIMAGES.COM/ PIPP

How to Use Your Inner Tools and Why Self Centeredness is a Good Thing FREEIMAGES.COM/RONIT GELLER

Chalk Board (less words) FREEIMAGES.COM/ILKER

Old Car – FREEIMAGES.COM/ KRISTEN SMITH

New Car – FREEIMAGES.COM/ANDY STAFINIAK

Send Them Into the Light - FREEIMAGES.COM/ ILONA KUUSELA

Removing the Energy Cords that Bind You
1. Picture of woman - FREEIMAGES.COM/ LOTUS HEAD
2. Energy Cords - FREEIMAGES.COM/DORA MITSONIA

Energy Cord Removal Process -
FREEIMAGES.COM/KIMBERLY VOHSEN

How to Call Your Purified Energy Back to You (telephone) -
FREEIMAGES.COM CRAIG YOUNG

Clear Your Space of Toxic Energy Debris –
FREEIMAGES.COM/ Antonio Jiménez Alonso

How the Subconscious Mind Works -
FREEIMAGES.COM MIRANDAKNOX

Stopping the Mind Chatter - FREEIMAGES.COM MAGDA S

Retraining the Mind-
1. Old mind – FREEIMAGES.COM KARL MOONEY
2. New Mind- FREE IMAGES.COM artM

How to use your emotions to shapeshift-
1. Caterpillar – FREEIMAGES.COM SCOTT CARTER
2. Butterfly - FREEIMAGES.COM JULIANA DIAS

How to Maintain a Positive Attitude & Raise Your Energetic Frequency- PIXABY.COM GERALT PUBLIC DOMAIN

Working with the Universe to Achieve Your Goals - PIXABY.COM GERALT PUBLIC DOMAIN

Visualization - How to Get Around the Blind Spots -
1. Eyes - FREEIMAGES.COM/INGRID MULLER
2. Peace sign in eyes - PIXABY.COM GERALT

Launching your intentions - PIXABY.COM SPACE-X IMAGERY PUBLIC DOMAIN

Other Tips and Tricks - PIXABY.COM ANIMATEDHEAVEN PUBLIC DOMAIN

Be What You Eat –
1.   Apples- PIXABY.COM JULENKA PUBLIC DOMAIN
2.   Oranges - PIXABY.COM INSPIREDIMAGES PUBLIC DOMAIN
3.   Oatmeal - FREEIMAGES.COM YAROSLAV B
4.   Grapes - PIXABY.COM MARKUS53 PUBLIC DOMAIN

All other images are from Adobe stock and I don't know who the photographers were.

About the Author

Psychic & Light Work Training Expert Rhonda Harris-Choudhry has been utilizing her psychic gifts since she was a teenager. She is a Goddess High Priestess and manifestation expert. Rhonda has made it her mission to empower people, particularly empaths by teaching them about their innate gifts and how to use them effectively to improve their health, life and happiness. She offers psychic readings and spiritual counseling as well as advanced psychic and healing training to practicing Light Workers and Metaphysicians. She also helps beginners to pin point and enhance their abilities as well as helping seasoned Light Workers to hone their skills.

You can view her website here: www.healinghennagoddess.com

Rhonda is a Goddess High Priestess of the Creation/Fertility Goddess spirituality. It is a part of her mission to help restore, increase and expand the Divine Feminine Energy in order to restore the Divine energetic balance in the world. She is the organizer for Goddess Spirituality and Learning Circle, an online meetup group that centers on Goddess based spirituality: http://www.meetup.com/GoddessSpiritualityCircle/

As a part of her mission to teach Empaths as well as all Metaphysicians how to stay healthy and happy, Rhonda creates free video trainings that can be viewed on her YouTube Channel. You can watch her training videos here (scroll to the second half of the page to view her playlists and click on the ones of interest): http://www.youtube.com/user/Azjua7/featured

As an Empath Training Expert and empath herself, Rhonda understands the challenges that empaths face and trains them in shielding and healing techniques to help them protect themselves. She also helps them identify and enhance the psychic gifts that come with being an empath.

As a Spiritual Counselor, Rhonda also offers empowerment psychic readings that help the client identify the true issues affecting them and offering positive resolutions to help them improve their situations. She also teaches her clients custom ways to manifest the things they desire in life.

As a Reiki Master and teacher, Rhonda uses her healing techniques to help heal you on multiple levels, emotionally, physically, mentally, spiritually as well as the energetic systems throughout the body. She also specializes in restoring balanced Goddess energy to women who have had to take on so many masculine roles that their feminine energy has suffered. By restoring their Divine Feminine strength and power, her clients leave feeling balanced, renewed and filled with Divine Feminine Power.

As a Past Life Regression therapist and Hypnotherapist, Rhonda helps people get in touch with their past lives to help them remember their past life spiritual teachings and/or to help them recognize where their fears and phobias come from. Using hypnotherapy, Rhonda is able to also help clients reprogram their subconscious to help bring create the life they want by ridding them of outdated and non-productive subconscious training that has held them back in life. Creating new subconscious beliefs helps to create new and productive lives for her clients.

Rhonda is also a psychic for Find Me, an organization of talented psychics, law enforcement officers and professional search and rescue volunteers from all over the world working with law enforcement and families to find missing loved ones and solve homicides. She co-wrote their advanced psychic training manual. https://www.findmegroup.org/

Please visit and like her Facebook Fan Page: https://www.facebook.com/GoddessRhonda/

Services:
Custom Intention manifestation training
Empowerment Psychic Readings including Power and Success readings and guidance
Spiritual Coaching
Empath and Psychic Training Classes
Metaphysics Training Classes
Distance Healing
Distance Spiritual Cleansings and Blessings
Past Life Regression

Custom meditations
Priestess Training
Training for various healing modalities, including Reiki, Auric Color
Therapy and more